Dyslexia:
Parents in Need

FAMILY FUTURES CONSORTIUM
35 Britannia Row
Islington, London, N1 8QH
TEL: 020 7354 4161 FAX: 020 7704 6200
A NOT FOR PROFIT ORGANISATION

Dyslexia:
Parents in Need

Pat Heaton

Whurr Publishers Ltd

© 1996 Whurr Publishers Ltd
First published 1996 by
Whurr Publishers Ltd
19b Compton Terrace, London N1 2UN, England

British Library Cataloguing in Publication Data
A catalogue record for this book is available from the British Library

ISBN 1-897635-73-7

Printed and bound in the UK by Athenaeum Press Ltd, Gateshead, Tyne & Wear

Contents

Foreword

Public interest in dyslexia or specific learning difficulty has increased substantially over the last decade, media coverage and so forth, leading to a more informed perception of the dyslexic's difficulties and needs. That children in need are a first consideration goes almost without saying, but it is important to remember that the dyslexic child does not live in a vacuum. His parents and family also have needs and these needs are very real.

I believe that the needs of parents are often forgotten; the professionals involved (psychologists, teachers and so on) prioritise the child's problems and, naturally, a parent's first concern is the dyslexic himself. Discussions usually focus on the child's needs; the needs of 'significant others' tend to remain unexpressed and sublimated. At least, long experience suggests that this is the case and from such impressions came the idea for this book, a book *by* parents, *for* parents, a text which allowed parents to speak directly to those in similar situations.

Of course, dyslexia-related problems do vary tremendously, but it seems to me that the parents of language-disabled children have much in common. For example, they generally want to know how to discriminate between significant and irrelevant symptoms and also how to help with both the academic and emotional aspects of dyslexia. Very importantly – in this context – they usually want to know about the day-to-day, practical management of the syndrome. As one father put it, 'I don't doubt that the professionals know what they're doing but I want to know from someone who's lived with it. It's no joke. I need to know how to help and how to survive dyslexia.'

This small book's aspirations, therefore, are very different from those of a reference or research document. It simply addresses a few of the main issues and tries to help parents to help themselves, their children and others similarly placed. Parents' responses to a questionnaire (see p. xi) inform the main text. The second section (guidelines and related word-searches/games) is a First Aid package which, in its unpublished form, has been used by numerous dyslexic students.

That parents have been both the resource and inspiration goes almost without saying; they have been generous not only with their time but also in sharing emotions and experiences. I can only hope that the finished product helps them as much as they have helped me.

Note: For he/his, read she/her if appropriate.

Introduction

That the term *dyslexia* means 'difficulty with words or language' is fairly well known. However, despite increasing public awareness of this and similar definitions, the condition's signs and symptoms are not always interpreted correctly. The syndrome seems to attract myths and misunderstandings. At first sight, this is rather surprising given the amount of literature on the subject, not to mention the various Dyslexia checklists[1] tests for home use and so forth.[2]

One problem, of course, is that dyslexia can show itself in many different ways and may arise from a number of causes. Difficulties with diagnosis are almost inevitable given the diversity of the symptoms. Having said that, dyslexics do share certain key characteristics. Primarily, they are all 'phonologically disabled' in the sense that they seem unaware that words consist of a number of different sounds which can be separated and rearranged. This, in turn, means that dyslexics have difficulties with reading, writing and spelling, hard evidence of a real problem. These linguistic problems can be observed in pupils who are otherwise performing perfectly well and the difficulties resist conventional instruction/remediation. A family history of language difficulty may also be significant.

Dyslexia is an enduring condition. It can affect many aspects of school and home life. The disability is both inconsistent and variable and discrepancies in performance are *normal* for the dyslexic pupil.

Notes
[1] See Awareness Information Sheet, British Dyslexia Association, 98 London Road, Reading, Berkshire, RG1 5AU.
[2] Inner Sense Development Centre, 39 Lickfold's Road, Farnham, Surrey, GU10 4AE.

The questionnaire

Working in the Special Needs field brings many rewards and advantages, amongst them opportunities for discussion with dyslexics and their families. Having said that, a mutual interest in dyslexia became something of a problem when I tried to classify the material for this little book; the sources and resources were almost too plentiful!

Fortunately – and not for the first time – a parent support group provided the solution to a problem. A questionnaire was suggested and I mentioned it to other parents in order to find out how people would feel about the idea.

As it happened, most were enthusiastic. Parents agreed to complete a questionnaire subject to certain conditions. All those involved agreed that questions should be open, that anonymity must be protected and that individuals should be free to express personal opinions. It was suggested that families currently involved in the diagnostic/statementing procedures should be excluded from the survey as 'experienced' parents had more to offer.

It was not difficult to design a questionnaire which accommodated these conditions and thirty parents took part in the survey. Their replies were detailed and – in many instances – illuminating. (I have permission to quote and edit as appropriate, and copies of some of the original responses are reproduced overleaf.)

Finally there is an unexpected bonus worth mentioning. Although most people reported some initial apprehension, more than half of the parents involved mentioned the therapeutic effects of completing the questionnaire. The experience appears to have helped some families to come to terms with dyslexia, and the questions (which also serve as a cross-reference for the first part of the book) are, therefore, reproduced below.

Questionnaire

1   What first made you think your child was different/was dyslexic?
     (See Chapter 1: Signs and symptoms: Early evidence).

2   Thinking of the language of the school-age and older child in particular, what can you remember?
     (See Chapter 2: Signs and symptoms: Language).

3a   How did you feel when you were told that your child was dyslexic?
3b   How has dyslexia affected family life?
     (See Chapter 3: Feelings, families and dyslexia).

4   What advice would you give to the parents of a child whose dyslexic condition has only recently been identified?
     (See Chapter 4: Help and advice: Method and management).

5   Thinking of the practical, day-to-day management of dyslexia, which strategies/resources/tactics have proved useful and why?
     (See Chapter 5: Dealing with the practicalities: Strategies/ resources/tactics).

Questionnaire: Samples of parent responses

The boys were sent home from school with word tins and reading books. Once the word tin contained more than a half dozen words the boys became confused and didn't recognise the words.

On open evenings at school I was shocked to see his writing books; the letters in words were all the wrong way around.

He would copy full pages from reading books but get some letters the wrong way round. When he wrote his own stories the words were grossly mis-spelt.

Sometimes he would be telling you something and although I new [sic] just what he was trying to say some of the words would come out all *back to front*. It is never 'left to right' with A_____ it is always 'right to left' – lots of other simple statements he says the 'wrong' way round.

My child was very forgetful and I thought it was for attention — unfortunately it wasn't. At school her words were spelt back to front.

Section One

Chapter 1
Signs and symptoms: Early evidence

Reference: Questionnaire item 1: What first made you think your child was different/was dyslexic?

Interestingly, the majority of parents involved in the survey felt 'Something wasn't quite right' long before their child started school. Although difficulties with the first reading book were often important tangible evidence of linguistic confusion, many parents recalled earlier signs and symptoms.

Variability and discrepancy of performance featured in the majority of responses: 'When he's tired he can jumble the letters in his own name but next day he can produce something brilliant from a few bits of Lego.'

To those unfamiliar with dyslexia what follows must sound paradoxical but unevenness of performance may be one of the condition's most reliable characteristics:

'So far as I was concerned, his reading did not match his vocabulary or intelligence.'

'I felt fairly sure that she was bright but I had to agree with her teacher; she could seem really slow with some things. Any instructions involving left and right had her completely baffled.'

'On "good days" he's brilliant; he's creative, imaginative and he even reads well – for him. Bad days, I try not to think about; he forgets how to tell the time, the reading regresses and altogether it seems like a waste of time and energy.'

Many parents said that they saw signs of a problem they could not describe long before their child started school. 'He had worked out the connection between plug, socket and video long before he could say a recognisable word. With his two brothers, it would have been the opposite way round.'

Parents who had tried to explain their intuitions to professionals had– more often that not – given up in confusion and/or embarrassment. A concerned and perplexed father described his frustration: 'In a way, I could understand why the school didn't believe us; he could produce beautiful work one day and the next– well, you wouldn't think it was the same child.'

Describing a visit to the doctor, one mother recalls:

> 'I really thought about it beforehand. I'd even written it down, I was so determined to get to the bottom of it. The trouble was – and I now realise this – that I wasn't telling him the right things. I kept on about his temper tantrums and bed-wetting but I never mentioned how bright he was in other ways.

With hindsight, the majority of parents recognise an unevenness of development in certain key areas. 'Something seemed to be missing; I knew he was "quick" in some ways but in others – and I have to say this – he could be really slow on the uptake compared with his younger brother.'

A father described a fairly typical situation. 'He loved listening to stories but he could never repeat the story-line. I *knew* he had understood every word I'd said, it was so frustrating.'

A grandma remembers noticing, 'She would look at the pictures rather than try to read. If I tried to interest her in the words she got down from my knee. I think it was all very confusing and frightening for her.'

Different dimensions of a dyslexic's behaviour puzzled another mother. 'He didn't need twice-telling when it came to helping on the farm but *dressing*!! He still puts things on back-to-front and upside-down.'

It seems then that any early unevenness in performance may be significant, especially if there exists a familial incidence of dyslexia. More particularly, evidence indicates that contrasts between general and linguistic development may be especially noteworthy.

> 'I felt sure that he understood but he was very late talking. I said it was because his sister did the talking for him but I was uneasy about it. It didn't seem natural.'

> 'He was so "up and down" with talking and we were all worried. He'd say a word one day and I'd tell his grandma –

she was as concerned as I was. Then when she came, it was just as though it had vanished while he was asleep. I used to wonder if people thought I was making it up – or if I was neurotic. It's a terrible position to be in.'

'She scrambled words: *car park* became *par cark*, *upstairs* became *stupstairs*, things like that.'

'He just couldn't remember nursery rhymes. He'd tell you the "story" in the rhyme but he just couldn't get the idea of how rhymes worked. I'd always thought it just came naturally so I was really puzzled.'

Given the dyslexic's innate phonological disability (mentioned earlier), the many reports of pre-school language problems were to be expected. As one father put it:

'He seems to have been slightly "out of sync" with language ever since he was born. He had speech problems, he couldn't articulate properly, couldn't understand what you were saying. And now, he's got problems with reading. What I'd like to understand is how a child with an Intelligence Quotient of 111 can be affected in so many different ways.'

Unfortunately, there are no easy answers in this situation. As has been mentioned, dyslexia can show itself in several different ways and at any level of language (decoding and encoding).

Having said that, experts believe that disparities in performance and other particular signs and symptoms of dyslexia relate to and are part of a *pattern of difficulties*. Problems with general competencies such as discrimination, sequencing, recall and orientation affect many different aspects of behaviour and performance. For instance, difficulty with understanding *instructions* connected with *directions* (orientation) was mentioned by a number of parents; it seems that left/right, back/front, up/down and so on are frequently confused.

Difficulty in recalling items in a *sequential order* was also mentioned frequently; an inability to recall story lines, days of the week, the alphabet, the order of garments when dressing appears to be common. Difficulty in *naming*, remembering the name of something or someone familiar or even the names of numbers is also characteristically dyslexic.

Thinking of the first signs of dyslexia in the pre-school child then, inexplicable failure in the tasks which require and develop these general competencies should be taken seriously. Many everyday activities (including speech) involve discrimination, orientation and accurate recall/sequencing skills. *Dressing* is a useful example; poor recall/unreliable ordering skills make dressing difficult; the child is unsure which item of clothing comes first – is it vest or pullover? If the child is further disabled by weak orientation (he can't tell his left from his right, for example) double-breasted items are a problem and dressing becomes a challenge rather than a routine.

Parents report that *uneven or late development* in these key areas proved to be significant; if a child has received an average amount of parental support/guidance, appears to be reasonably intelligent in many ways, but continues to have a more than average difficulty with language and/or a substantial proportion of the type of tasks described, a diagnosis of dyslexia may well be appropriate. In other words, to return to an earlier theme, variability and disparity should not be treated lightly.

> 'I thought she was being forgetful on purpose, that it was a form of attention seeking. I didn't interpret the signs, I couldn't see what was causing the problem. Once I realised what a shocking memory she had I began to work out the effects for myself. It's frightening.'

> 'The family said that he was lazy but I know now that it wasn't that; he truly couldn't cope with the things I asked him to do. Now I understand it's all so obvious.'

Experiments and formal investigations confirm parental perceptions. Miles (1993)[1] has long argued in favour of early investigation of a 'pattern of difficulties' and more recent developments include a computer program[2] geared to pre-school screening and early recognition of dyslexia.

Reviewing the available evidence, it appears that parents and psychologists are saying the same: that although problems with reading may be the first tangible evidence of dyslexia, the well-informed will recognise other traits long before the child starts school.

Finally, to conclude this chapter, it is worth saying that most of the parents involved in this survey wished they had trusted their instincts. An overwhelming majority felt that some professionals had too readily dismissed early expressions of concern.

Note

[1]   Miles, T., *Understanding Dyslexia,* Teach Yourself Books.

[2]   Lucid Systems Ltd, Research Centre, Hull University, Hull.

Chapter 2
Signs and symptoms: Language

Reference: Questionnaire item 2: Thinking of the language of the school-age and older child in particular, what can you remember?

That language and learning are intertwined is obvious and – with hindsight – many of the parents interviewed realised that the 'muddlement' and variability associated with dyslexia/specific learning difficulty were both obvious at an early stage of their child's development (see Chapter 1). Evidence from parents also suggests that the older dyslexic's language development – more often than not – continues to display all the signs and symptoms of the fundamental weaknesses apparent at the pre-school stage:

> 'He would move his finger along the line but his finger and the word rarely corresponded. Sometimes he'd start by pointing at the far right hand side of the page . . . he'd obviously no notion of how it all worked.'

> 'They had flash cards for the reading scheme at school and she could not remember the simplest words, however much we practised. . . You could hold them upside down and she didn't know the difference!'

It goes almost without saying that reports of problems with discrimination/orientation/sequencing/recall were numerous and it was felt that these difficulties affected all aspects of language in one way or another. Having said that, and for convenience, each aspect of language development is treated separately here, speech being considered first.

Signs and symptoms: speech: a few examples from parents:

A 14-year-old girl, identified as dyslexic by a Local Education Authority's psychologist, complained 'He keeps telling me to pull my socks out.' The same girl, discussing a risky initiative, said that she saw no need, 'To stick my nose out.'

Referring to a *word-search* set for homework, a 9-year-old is reported as saying, 'I like those *search-words*, they're OK.'

A similar sort of innate difficulty is apparent in a teenager's utterance: 'I put the milk of bottle back in the fridge.'

Families of dyslexic children will recognise the Spoonerisms which are associated with dyslexia/specific learning difficulty.

A reported conversation with a 10-year-old who has been formally assessed as, 'moderately dyslexic with an average intelligence', was revealing. Talking about hanging baskets of flowers he apparently volunteered that, 'We have two in the back of the house, each side of the front door.'

A few minutes conversation and all the signs and symptoms were obvious but Sam's utterances could give a false impression of his skills and abilities. His reason for not buying a particular game for his computer was fascinating: 'It was too much less than a lot so it can't have been any good.'

Another young dyslexic, talking about his school's proposed coach trip to Wales, said that the journey would take, 'From six to five hours depending on the traffic'.

Many parents were of the opinion that this awkwardness with language must affect learning and development. It certainly puts Sam and children like him in a vulnerable position; they may be perceived as foolish or even mentally handicapped. The popular belief that fluent speech, reading and writing all come 'naturally' does not help the dyslexic's case. That language acquisition is not a problem for most children is obvious but dyslexics *are* different.

An adult dyslexic (who has an Honours Degree in computer technology) explained how the syndrome affects his speech and fluency:

> 'As I see it, it takes two different but related forms. I have a sort
> of internal dictionary and it contains everything I can put a
> name to. The trouble is that I can't always find exactly what I
> want but I know it's there and that on another day I would
> most probably go straight to it.

For example, I might want to say, "Hand me the steps", but I might say, "Pass me the ladder", because on that day I could find the concept for the item I wanted (a barred structure, used for climbing) but not its precise label.'

Category errors like this affect communication skills and limit self-expression.

Other equally frustrating experiences were also recounted:

'Another time the problem may be quite different: verbs and grammar can be especially awkward. Even now, I might find the word I'm after but struggle to organise it grammatically; irregular verbs are still a problem. On a bad day I could still say, 'I was intentioned to do it last night but I forgot.'

This young man's Intelligence Quotient is 130+ and he was assessed as being 'severely dyslexic'. He did not start to read until he was nine. His reading speed is still below average and he constantly checks that he has not misunderstood a speaker's message.

Not every dyslexic has to cope with such an extreme degree of difficulty but clearly, verbal inaccuracy and awkwardness should be taken seriously.

Signs and symptoms: reading

A few of the parents involved in this survey said that they could have predicted their child's reading failure and several stated that this hard evidence of underlying disabilities was the first step on the road to recognition and remediation.

It is commonly recognised that reading is a highly complex activity: it seems both to require and develop sub-skills such as perception, orientation, sequencing and recall (see p. 3). The fluent reader is believed to have moved smoothly through a three-stage process:

- Logographic stage – the child sees the word holistically; words are pictures;
- Alphabetic stage – the child appreciates the significance of sound/letter correspondence;
- Orthographic stage – the child uses both logographic and alphabetic strategies when reading and spelling.

Research suggests that the typical dyslexic gets stuck at either the first or second stage.

To appreciate some of the complexities of both process and disability is to begin to understand the reasons for failure; in this case, the whole is almost certainly more than the sum of the parts. For example: if the child cannot distinguish between left and right, back and front, and so forth, he may be totally confused by the layout of the page. Should he start from the bottom or from the top? Should he read from right to left or vice versa? Does it matter? (In a sense, it doesn't, if he is still at the logographic stage.) Where should he start if he has to build the word – in the middle, on the right or on the left? (If he starts anywhere, he does not understand the significance of sound/letter ordering and matching.)

Moreover, the pupil with specific learning difficulties may not perceive differences between: b/d, m/w, n/u, p/9, g/q. Reports of word reversals are common (reading *on* as no, for example) as are instances of difficulties with labelling. (The child may recognise a word but fail to find the correct label or forget its name – see page 6).

The business of converting abstractions (letters/the written word) into meaning, into something that can be identified in the real world, must seem tremendously complicated to a dyslexic. The fact that almost everyone else appears to read with ease and fluency does not help matters.[1]

Parents provided many specific illustrations of reading errors and the following examples may be of interest;

Written word (the stimulus):   Child's response

Written word (the stimulus)	Child's response
boots	boost
until	unite
tell	let
area	rare
assumed	amused
over	very
cast	cats
but	put
spilling	slipping
but	tub
dressed	distressed
gave	very
chocolate	school

[1]   Readers concerned with research theory may be interested in Snowling's model of the reading process. See *Children's Language Difficulties*, NFER/Nelson.

aching arms	aching legs
darkness	blackness
the	and
I	A
I	you
men	people
short	small
Double Scotch	Double Whisky
metal	iron
shed	hut
drink	milk
amazement	astonishment

Close examination of these errors is revealing. In some instances, development appears to be arrested at the logographic stage; (visual stimulus *the* provokes the response *and*, the logograph *Double Scotch* is read as *Double Whisky*, for example). In other cases, the child seems to know something about sound/letter matching and ordering but poor perceptual/sequencing/orientation/recall skills affect performance; (a possible explanation for *boots* provoking the response *boost*).

Many other instances of the dyslexic's tendency to 'mis-cue' were provided by parents; the selection will perhaps give some idea of the scale of the problem.

Signs and symptoms: spelling (writing)

Given that spelling and reading are interrelated (though independent) skills, it follows that the problems with reading are almost always accompanied (or followed) by difficulties with spelling. There seems to be a connection between reading and spelling styles; the child who is stuck at the logographic or alphabetic stage of reading is unlikely to be good at spelling.

It is also important to remember that – spelling tests apart – an exclusive focus on spelling is rare. More usually, the child is simultaneously preoccupied with planning, ideas, punctuation, grammar and so forth. That the dyslexic's inherent weaknesses become very apparent in free writing is hardly surprising.

Many examples of written work (see pp. 10–11) were supplied by parents of identified dyslexics. The very obvious difficulties with spelling and so on may account for some of the frustrations expressed by these pupils, *none of whom has a less than average measured intelligence.*

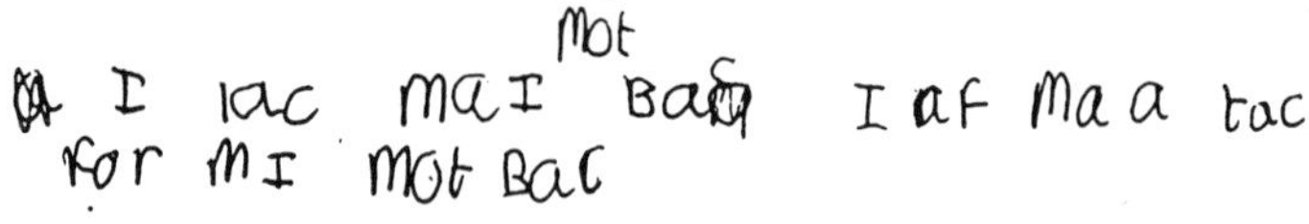

[handwritten sample]

Andrew, 9 years

(I like my motor bike. I have made a track for my motor bike.)

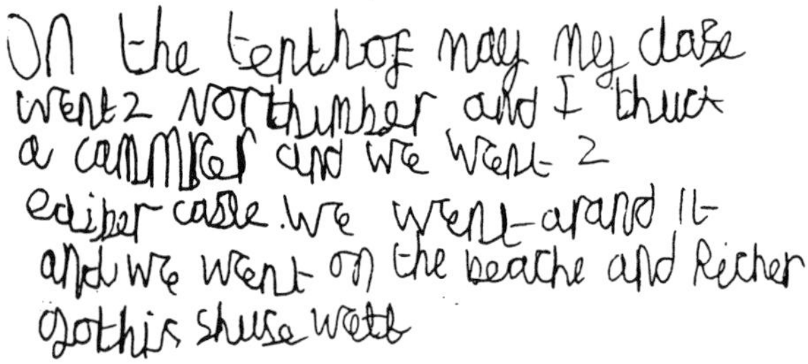

[handwritten sample]

Robert, 9 years

(On the tenth of May my class went to Northumberland and I took a camera and we went to Edinburgh Castle we went around it and we went on the beach and Richard got his shoes wet.)

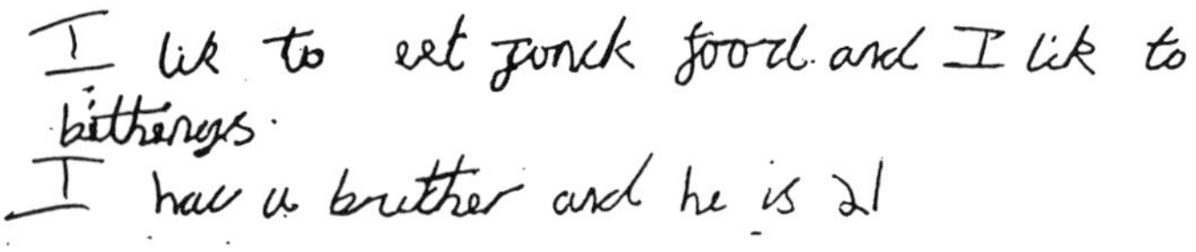

[handwritten sample]

Lewis, 11 years

(I like to eat junk food and I like to buy things. I have a brother and he is 21.)

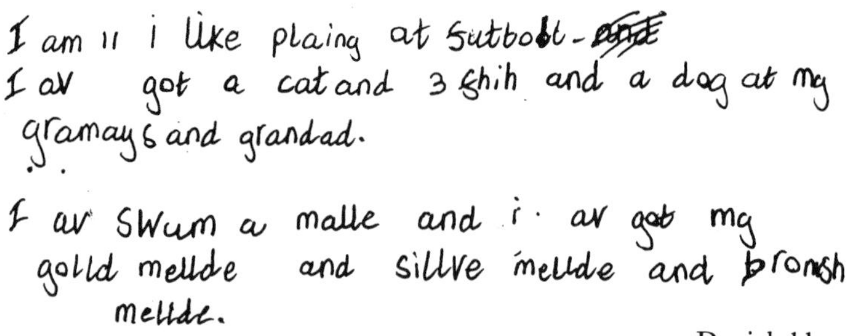

[handwritten sample]

Daniel, 11 years

(I am 11. I like playing at football. I have got a cat and 3 fish and a dog at my grandma's and grandad.

I have swum a mile and I have got my gold medal and silver medal and bronze medal.)

My Faverate hobby is playing on my ~~comp~~ compute and my Game Gare. My faverete came is sonic II. My faverate Gaame for my computer is Senceble Soccor. I also like going to watch barnsley play Football

Richard, 13 years

(My favourite hobby is playing on my computer and my game gear. My favourite game is Sonic II. My favourite game for my computer is Sensible Soccer. I also like going to watch Barnsley play football.)

At School we are playing Football the last time we played a I got my atrick well the team we where playing whent all that good we could have won about 100 - 0 but we ownly won the game. 25-0 the ball was never in one ① owe ② hafe. Next week I hope we play a harder ③ tram So we can have ⑤ Soorce. will good fa match. and the a drow but it is not be 25-0 it ⑥ mint be P.T.O.

a game so i do not ⑥ caese we ⑦ how win the game.

1. hoer
2. half
3. team
4. Scoor
5. mint
6. caire
7. ~~how~~ hwo

Paul, 12 years

Paul's work at age 12. He identified seven spelling mistakes himself and attempted to correct them.

Signs and symptoms: writing: conclusion

All the extracts contain examples of typically dyslexic difficulties and clearly even the shortest piece of free writing is a potential minefield for a dyslexic. The extracts also demonstrate that levels of literacy, academic achievement and intelligence do not *always* go hand-in-hand, that there are many and significant exceptions[1] to this general 'rule'.

Signs and symptoms: listening

It is difficult to assess listening skills but assuming that the majority find it easier to read than to write, it probably follows that a listener's role is easier than that of a speaker; the former does not have to organise his vocabulary, ideas, grammar, and so forth. The respondent merely has to make sense of the message. Compared with the speaker's situation, the listener's role is easy, relatively passive rather than active.

Having said that, given the innate disabilities described earlier, the dyslexic's listening skills will, presumably, be inferior when compared with those of his peers. Listening (making sense of the message) is not so easy if you are dyslexic. Reports from parents support this conclusion:

> 'It seems to take him that long sometimes, before the message sinks in. I sometimes wonder if it goes round twice.'

> 'I can understand why his teachers run out of patience: he looks so blank at times that you wonder if you've started talking Martian!'

> 'I've known me give an instruction, she's repeated it after me and then *she's done it wrong!*'

> 'I have to be honest and admit that I find it vastly irritating, at times. If it's anything more than one item or a very simple instruction, we have problems.'

Many parents said (in one way or another) that they had learned the importance of *the order of mention*:

> 'I give instructions in the order that I want them carried out.

---

[1] Readers interested in learning more about famous dyslexics should consult Dr Hornsby's text, *Overcoming Dyslexia*, Dunitz.

That means I have to think before I open my mouth! I try never to say things like, "and while you're doing that": it guarantees failure and confusion!'

A father made a similar comment:

'You can never just say something, in passing; you have to check that she's really concentrating, find time to ask her to repeat it in the same order and then check again. I couldn't just ask her to nip upstairs and get a couple of things, like I might ask you. I'd have to check that she was really concentrating.'

By contrast, the average listener is very competent, almost without trying. Even when he is not actively involved in listening, an echo of the utterance is available for reference. He gets the message: the information is processed and any necessary action is initiated; he has no difficulty distinguishing between what is vital and what is irrelevant.

Also, some educationalists believe that listening skills are declining generally and that attention depends increasingly on visual stimulation. Whether or not this is so, listening skills feature in the National Curriculum. One local authority's programme of study says that listening activities should 'help to develop in pupils' speaking and listening their grasp of sequencing, cause and effect, reasoning, sense of consistency, clarity of argument, appreciation of relevance and irrelevance, and powers of recall and prediction'. Another local authority suggests that evidence of listening skills should 'demonstrate an ability to internalise and interpret then convey a message to appropriate person'. Obviously, these objectives are laudable but most parents had doubts about their child's chances of success in this area.

A dyslexic's sister explained, 'I always wait until he's unscrambled the first bit before I go any further; sometimes he just seems to lose interest; I'm sure it's something to do with him being dyslexic'. Another explanation for the dyslexic's poor listening skills was offered by a grandad. 'I know kids can play you up but I honestly think he finds listening hard work; what comes naturally to us is hard work to him. I think he stops concentrating because he's worn out.' Personal experience indicates that improved listening and improved literacy do tend to go together, but many parents were unsure about this. On balance, it is perhaps fair to say that listening is no more natural than reading for some dyslexics.

Signs and symptoms: language: conclusion

It is impossible to quantify the effects of language retardation on learning but presumably each has an effect on the other. Certainly most psychologists feel that the two are intertwined and given this, the pupil experiencing dyslexic-type difficulties will probably be at a disadvantage in a (largely) language-based school environment.

Summarising then, he may have difficulties with any of the following language-based activities:

- reading and spelling;
- poor organisation of written work;
- misunderstanding of instructions;
- copying from the board;
- explaining/describing anything – including himself!

All or any of these different aspects of school life may be affected by inherent language disability, the dyslexic's real potential frequently being obscured by linguistic 'muddlement'.

This, of course, is what parents and dyslexics find so very frustrating!

Chapter 3
Feelings, families and dyslexia

Reference: Questionnaire items 3a) and 3b):
3a) How did you feel when you were told that your child was dyslexic?
3b) How has dyslexia affected family life?

To appreciate that relief is sometimes the first reaction to a diagnosis of dyslexia is to begin to understand the worries and fears experienced by many parents of dyslexic children. Diagnosis often comes after months or in some cases, years of anxiety and frustration; it is therefore not so surprising that the identification or labelling of the problem sometimes comes as a relief. 'I was so relieved to know that it had a name', said one mother who recognised that she had been a victim of her own imagination.

Such responses are not uncommon. It seems that for many people not knowing is worse than knowing. Having said that, several fathers had apparently experienced very mixed feelings when investigations began – especially if they were themselves dyslexic. Similarly, every mother involved in the survey had been fearful, but determined.

'I was scared to death of what they might tell me but I knew we couldn't go on ignoring the fact that he couldn't read. Whatever they said though, *any* diagnosis had got to be better than this never-ending thinking about what had caused it.'

That the pain and vulnerability of parents is very real is obvious:

'When he couldn't get going with reading I thought he had a brain tumour.'

'I had been nagging for two years to try and find out what was wrong, but nobody would listen. . . I was worried sick about how she'd survive in secondary . . . they all promised but nobody *did* anything. The assessment was the best thing that had happened in months!'

'When they told me he was clever but dyslexic, I could have cried. It was such a relief to know that it could be treated.'

'My family had begun to hint that she might be mentally retarded because she was illiterate. I could never explain why I knew she wasn't so the diagnosis helped me a lot.'

Many parents described early attempts to explain something they themselves didn't understand and residual bitterness is not unusual. One parent said she felt very angry when she was finally told that her son was dyslexic. 'The people who should have been helping me fobbed me off . . . he should have been assessed and helped earlier . . . they pretended they didn't know what I was talking about.'

Bitterness, anger and guilt were mentioned frequently when parents recalled what they felt when they discovered their child was dyslexic:

'All those years trying to bully and bribe him into reading . . . I felt so guilty.'

'It was a relief but I also felt very guilty as if I'd let her down. I knew she was intelligent, you see. When she forgot things I thought it was on purpose, for attention.'

'It's difficult enough being a parent these days but when you're told they're dyslexic, you wonder how you'll cope. You also wonder if it's your fault in some way.'

'I suspected that I might be dyslexic myself so I had very mixed feelings about it all, guilt I suppose. My wife's had a lot to put up with, with two of us. . . I knew what he was going through as well but, at that stage, I couldn't see how diagnosis and assessment could help. I know better now, of course. Diagnosis means he's getting the right treatment though I still feel it's my fault that we've had all these problems.'

That difficulties with literacy and numeracy might also affect behaviour was a revelation to a number of parents:

'What the psychologist said made a lot of sense to me. I suppose it's obvious but I didn't think of it. His ego's bound to be fragile and that's why he's so difficult to handle. When she explained all the other things about dyslexia, I began to understand what was going on better. I began to understand myself as well – from what she said, I think I'm dyslexic so I've had to do some rethinking on my own behalf . . . it's not been easy.'

Post-mortems and analysis seem to be a common consequence of assessment and diagnosis:

'We discussed it for hours, days, we couldn't leave it alone. It brought all sorts of things into the open, things we'd never talked about before.'

'Once we'd read the report, I couldn't stop thinking about it. It explained such a lot, not only about his problems with spelling but about his bad temper. And I have to admit – in the first instance – each of us blamed the other.'

For some families, exchanges like this may be a necessary part of coming to terms with the disability. Having said that, many parents said that they regretted that stage, seeing it as damaging to family relationships and – most importantly – unhelpful to their child.

Then again, a positive aspect was identified:

'At least the problem was well and truly aired and all the family knew about it.'

'We felt very much on our own at that stage but in a funny sort of way that was good . . . it made us closer . . . we both knew we had to pull together . . . nobody else was going to help . . . we had to share the responsibility.'

The degree of familial support to be expected after diagnosis appears to vary considerably and the involvement of extended family and friends seems to be a mixed blessing. Apparently, a problem shared is not necessarily a problem halved!

'There are only two members of my family who know, I haven't told any of my husband's family because they would make a big issue of it.'

'Family and friends tried to be helpful but they didn't really understand.'

'Mixed reactions from my family, some still say she is a late developer.'

'Friends tended to react as though it was some sort of conta-
gious life-threatening disease.'

Hurt feelings arising from lack of understanding are mentioned
frequently though most parents seem to manage to forgive and
forget the past, eventually.

By contrast, for some families the debate about 'labelling' never
ends. Many parents perceived both advantages and disadvantages in
labelling a child dyslexic: a number of parents pointed out that
although a particular teacher's (or in later years, employer's)
response may be quite positive, this type of reaction cannot be generally assumed. (A prospective employer, for example, might well reject
the dyslexic candidate in favour of what he sees as a better specula-
tion.)

Generally speaking, parents disliked the idea of a permanent
label but appreciated the advantages of assessment and diagnosis.
'Now I look back, I can see it was the beginning of the end although
I don't like the labelling.' Responses like this were typical and
certainly the majority of parents involved in this survey saw formal
recognition as informing and precipitating the long looked-for
specialist remediation.

Perhaps equally important, a positive diagnosis of dyslexia appears
to promote confidence and assertiveness. Given a label, parents
seemed more inclined to do their own research and to read up on the
subject. 'I know what I'm talking about now. I don't much care what
they call it so long as they get on and do something about it.'

Such robust attitudes are not unusual. A few parents believed that
any negative consequences of labelling the child dyslexic were small
compared with the advantages.

'As soon as I knew it had a name I felt better.'

'We had a focus then, before that we'd wondered about everything and anything.'

Generally speaking, parents felt that labelling was recognition and
that one was a consequence of the other. Certainly, diagnosis and
recognition had, in the first instance, been a tremendous relief to
confused and worried parents.

Having said this, it is important to remember that recognition is
only a step along the way, so to speak. The interactive and extensive
nature of the innate disabilities causes many problems, some more
obvious than others (see Chapters 1 and 2). Assessment and diagnosis
merely identify the disability; they do not cure it.

Reference: Questionare item 3b):

How has dyslexia affected family life?

Replies to this enquiry will probably be of particular interest to parents of children very recently identified as dyslexic. Responses tended to revolve around three interrelated themes. Some parents compared attitudes and behaviour before and after diagnosis/tuition whereas others described some practical problems associated with dyslexia. All parents mentioned the cost and/or other consequences of specialist remediation.

> 'I know we're very lucky, we're not paying for the teaching but it still costs, in other ways. We have to remind her about doing her "special homework" and I think sometimes that the other two must get fed up of all this fuss about dyslexia but I don't see how you can avoid it.'

> 'Private tuition has put a strain on finances which would other-wise have been used for holidays/pleasure. Having said that, it's been worth every penny.'

> 'We have to keep Saturday morning free for her to have private tuition; if there had been more real help in school and they recognised the problem, it would have saved our family budget about £14 per week.'

> 'It's sometimes a strain to keep up with the extra tuition both from the financial and the supervisory point of view. Home-work can be a real battle. My wife and I both work full-time and homework can be the last straw. Basically, the dyslexia takes time, energy and money we can't really afford. On the other hand, I can really see a difference in him.'

Not surprisingly, most parents were unhappy about having to pay for private tuition; the majority of parents interviewed here were also unhappy with their particular local education authority.

> 'We are very disappointed in the local education system. If you want anything special, you have to fight very hard and wait a long time to get anything done. Fighting for recognition and tuition caused a lot of stress . . . I was forever having to take time off to go to school for meetings and one thing and another. The specialist tuition should be more freely avail-able.'

'I don't really believe in private education but what else can you do? We were getting desperate. He had absolutely no confidence in himself, he was so desperate to please, it was pitiful. It got to the stage where his dyslexia was affecting everything. We were becoming an "at risk" family.'

That many dyslexics feel diminished by poor literacy skills is not surprising. Reading and spelling are usually central to success in the education system; if a pupil cannot keep up with his or her peers in this respect, he will probably have a poor self concept. That this is not unusual is shown by the following extracts from questionnaire responses:

Before Diagnosis and/or Tuition:

'Very quiet with all members of the family. When we used to visit my sister he would just sit there, quiet and nervous until we went home. I used to make excuses for him . . . I feel awful now when I think what I put him through, but I didn't see a connection between his poor school work and his shyness.'

'He was shy even with relatives and close friends. He found conversation really difficult. I was forever trying to bring him into the conversation but when I managed it, half the time I'd wish I hadn't; he'd say something that made sense only to me.'

'She was so inhibited and seemed to cry at nothing: that's not a bit like our family. She seemed to get swamped by it all, she hated the Sunday tea-party at my mother's. I couldn't understand it.'

After Diagnosis and/or Tuition:

'He's much friendlier when visiting. I suppose he's more confident, he's up and down playing with different things. He's more talkative, wants to know what's what. He actually sings to himself, I can't tell you how marvellous it is to hear it. I honestly think we're a happier family now that we know what it is we are dealing with.'

'He now enjoys the company of the family and close friends. He likes to show them the work he has done with his specialist tutor and the models he makes. It is obvious that he is much more confident.'

'I can't quite explain it. She's sort of much more light-hearted; before we knew what the problem was, life was so very serious. Now I think about it, it must have seemed very confusing. Now that she's happier we're all happier. If she's had a bad day – been put down a lot – we all have a 'scratchy' evening.'

Most families have problems at one time or another and dyslexia is an added complication. On occasions, dealing with dyslexia seems to stretch resources (finances, energy and so on) to the limit. In this situation, even the most patient parent feels under pressure:

'It drives me crazy at times. I've got three dyslexics to deal with: my husband and both children are dyslexic . . . I'm the only one with a memory . . . well that's how it feels. Quite seriously, one way and another dyslexia has put our marriage and family life under a lot of stress. I know there are worse things and other mothers tell me it'll all be worth it but can you imagine how shattered I am when they've all gone out in the morning? They all have to be reminded about what they need that day . . . and then I've to go to work.'

That occasional irritation is an inevitable consequence of daily dealings with dyslexia was confirmed by every participating parent:

'Getting organised in a morning can be a nightmare. I know all about colour-coding the calendar so that a green Tuesday means he has to take his green swimming trunks but there's a lot more to it than that. I think that he honestly does try but he forgets where things are and sometimes the patience just runs out.'

'If we're running late it's a disaster . . . everything goes from bad to worse. He always ties his shoelaces in a funny way but if we're late it gets even more convoluted. Even the language goes, under pressure . . . I have to try to seem calm or he'll never be able to find the name of what it is he's to take . . . I'll have to guess what "a thingy" is!'

It was ages before I could delegate anything; I couldn't send him to the shop because he'd come back with the wrong things; I couldn't ask him to phone my mother for me because he'd ring the wrong number or give her the wrong message. Of course, when he began to take some responsibility it seemed marvellous . . . I never take it for granted.'

'Dyslexia's limited her independence. At 14, she ought to be able to go into town on her own but she's nervous about it. I understand it but I sometimes run out of patience . . . it doesn't help that we live between B — — and D — — and that the numbers on the front of the buses are very similar. She once got on the wrong bus and had to walk home . . . you can imagine the effect of that!'

Responses like this give some idea of the ways in which family life is affected by what has been called 'a hidden handicap'. The description appears to be very appropriate; the problems are real but they are not always tangible and this can be frustrating. As one father said:

'If you could see something everybody would be more helpful. He *is* profoundly disabled but it isn't obvious. Having a poor memory, for example, *is* disabling in all sorts of different ways – practical and educational. I get sick and tired of trying to explain, of having to fight every step of the way. And I have to admit, I forget myself. I think I'd have more patience if I could *see* something. It would be a reminder of what it's like for him.'

The whole that is dyslexia is clearly far more than the sum of its parts. Although parents recognised the positive side of diagnosis and tuition, they also felt that dealing with dyslexia had not improved the quality of family life; many potentially irritating aspects of the disability were believed to be exacerbated by the stresses and strains of modern living. A number of parents felt that their tolerance, energy and drive fell short of what was required and all said that they had felt guilty about this at one time or another.

Two fathers who are themselves dyslexic expressed a very particular sort of guilt:

'On top of our son's problems, my wife has to help me. I'm self-employed *and* dyslexic. My wife has to help me with the books, with letters and quotes, with spelling . . . with almost everything except the practical side of the business. I don't know that dyslexia's done either of us any good. If I'm honest, I think we've both resented my dependence at times but without her the family just wouldn't function – at any level.'

'I know my wife takes more responsibility than she should have to. She sorts out all the family's organisational problems. When it comes down to it, I'm not much better than my son... I do try to teach him the few strategies I've learnt myself, but there never seems to be enough time.'

Perhaps every parent of a disabled/handicapped child experiences this at some time; to balance professional, domestic and other commitments is in itself no small task and any complication increases the pressure on both the individual and the family. Any 'handicap' in a member of the family creates additional problems.

Furthermore, expectations affect behaviour; the expectations of parents, siblings and so on tend to be based on norms and some families find accommodating abnormal behaviour harder than others. Coping with dyslexia is – in this respect – little different from dealing with other handicaps and each handicap has its own characteristics. However, these characteristics are often fairly obvious and that is perhaps a key issue here. The dyslexic's weaknesses are *not* immediately obvious or classifiable. Furthermore, his way of dealing with the demands of home and school may be particularly idiosyncratic and/or irritating; he is coping with many interacting disabilities. That dyslexia substantially affects family life in many different ways is obvious. Maybe the dyslexic's family too should be recognised as disabled and disadvantaged.

Chapter 4
Help and advice:
Method and
management

Reference: Questionnaire item 4: What advice would you give to the parents of a child whose dyslexic condition has only recently been identified?

Clearly, it is impossible to offer advice to suit every age, stage and circumstance but many parents drew general conclusions from their personal experiences. Both awareness and organisation were seen as central to the successful management of dyslexia. Managing paperwork and procedures, awareness and development, dealing with teaching and emotions were the main themes here.

First then, regarding the paperwork involved in making the case for recognition, assessment and (perhaps) statementing,[1] all parents were unprepared for its volume and complexity.

'What I would say is, create a system or it'll drive you crazy. I was always losing things and that just adds to the pressure. It caused rows in our house.'

'Make a filing system: photocopy everything and keep a diary. Don't rely on your memory; this is probably going to go on a long time and you're bound to forget the one thing you need. Remember, you're dealing with professionals and they probably have their own filing clerk – and filing system – for a very good reason!'

'Be prepared to spend time and energy on letter writing, filling in forms and that sort of thing. You'll be amazed by how much

---

[1] Statementing procedures deal with formal recognition/provision by the Local Education Authority. Copies of the current *Code of Practice on the Identification and Assessment of Special Educational Needs* can be obtained from Department for Education and Employment, Sanctury Buildings, Great Smith Street, West minster, London SW1P 3BT.

there is and you'll not see the point of a lot of it. That's one of the reasons I got so frustrated but I do know now that I'd have coped better if I'd allowed more time . . . it's a job in itself . . . you can't just tuck it in somewhere between washing up and cleaning up. Sometimes it took me a whole morning to get a set of papers together.'

The advantages of being proactive were mentioned by several parents, many of whom had made contacts at both local and national level:

'Join the local dyslexia organisation or mothers' support group. That way you'll get both support and information . . . my local group helped and encouraged me such a lot . . . the thing is, you're benefiting from the experience of those who've been there. Without help, I'd never have got to grips with the statementing procedure'. (See footnote 1 on p.24.)

Getting myself on the governors really paid off and getting elected is not as hard as you might think. Once you're on you're right at the centre of it. You know what they're supposed to be doing.'

'Find out about training courses. Some institutions will take you on even if you're not a teacher. It really is worth the effort and the money. I did an awareness course at my local college. If yours doesn't have one, ask if they'll consider it. I learned such a lot in a short time . . . about the teaching, about why he acts as he does . . . it was really helpful.'

'Start networking. Write off to any organisation that has any connection with dyslexia. Once you're on their mailing list you'll get all the latest information. You don't have to buy services and products but you can pick up a lot of incidental and free information from advertising packs.

'I did the Open University unit on Specific Learning Difficulty/Dyslexia and I've never looked back. It's given me so much confidence in so many different ways. I know I'm much better informed than I was . . . I suppose that's why I'm so assertive about his and my rights these days.'

Advice about teaching, homework and education in general also featured prominently in parents' replies:

'Get some teaching organised. Go privately if you have to –

talk to your local association – we had a private tutor at first because the LEA took so long. It was money well spent. She made terrific progress. Also, it meant we knew what we were looking for when we were offered help in school.'

Many parents had learned that the appropriateness of methods and remediation should not be assumed. 'Find out about the first principles of teaching dyslexics. I took everything for granted and, of course, he didn't make much progress; we had spent six months doing more of the same – but slower!'

That multi-sensory methods and structured phonic language programmes are best for dyslexics is well established, but the terminology had initially defeated at least two of the mothers involved in this survey:

'Find out what it means. It's not that difficult once you get down to it. Basically, it's lots of repetition and lots of different ways of doing the same thing. Ask the teacher if you can sit in; I found that really helpful and it means I'm better at helping with the homework.'

'If you find out what it's all about you'll know what to look for. You want a fully qualified specialist who really understands everything about dyslexia. He had a 'baby sitter' until I realised what was going on. . . Keep an eye on the homework, you'll learn a lot about all sorts of things.'

A number of parents had an eye to the future:

'Make sure that every teacher knows he's dyslexic. It can make all the difference when it comes to streaming and setting. If you're like me you'll find that you have to go into school several times before you're satisfied. I don't know how it happens but at every parents' evening I used to find at least one teacher who was totally unaware of his problems' (see Chapter 5, pp. 29–30).

'As soon as he's in secondary, start thinking about exams, what concessions might be available, what resources he might need. You need to know what the options are, whether it's to do with exams, training courses or further and higher education. You might even think he should be registered as disabled. The point is, you'd be well advised to start thinking early because everything takes so long. It can be very frustrating.'

That the dyslexic himself is often frustrated and emotional is hardly surprising given the largely literacy-based school environment. Strenuous effort may not be rewarded and emotional outbursts are common. Families recognised this and suggested different ways of coping with the many causes and effects of frustration.

'Try not to take over-reactions to heart. The frustration has to come out somewhere and home's the best place. If he's going to stab the paper with his pen, he's better doing it at the kitchen table.'

'Try and get him to talk about it; bottling it up is not a good idea. I can remember J — getting beside himself about really trivial things and finding out later that something had happened at school.'

'I've always encouraged other kids in the class to come round. It's good for all sorts of reasons, not least because you get a better idea of what's going on, a better perspective. Don't *ever* spring into action on the strength of your child's report of an incident/grievance. Talk first and always remember that there are children with worse – but – different problems.'

Compensating for language-based failures was a priority for several parents:

'You must re-build their confidence. We had to find something that she did really well and even better than other children her age. It wasn't easy but we encouraged her to try anything she fancied and eventually we found that she excelled in things like art. We bought her books, took her to some exhibitions, even arranged for a few lessons on perspective. We never thought she was going to be another Picasso but it helped boost her ego.'

'Make a positive effort to find time to listen, even if it means a bit of reorganisation. Listening's a priority and you shouldn't insult him by half-listening while you're doing something else. He gets enough insults – one way and another – at school.

'Even when you're tired yourself you *must* support and encourage. You might have had a bad day but think what they've had to put up with. If you think about it, while they're in school they're failing almost all the time and there's no prospect of escape from either the failure or the environment. Imagine how desperate you'd feel if your job were like that.'

Managing the emotional turmoils of a dyslexic and a family as well is not easy and an ongoing battle about provision does not help matters. It is easy to see why dyslexia could become a full-time pre-occupation. Two parents had learned from bitter experience:

'Don't get obsessive about it – I did and it's a mistake. It's better for all concerned if you don't get too emotional about it. If you're really desperate about some hurt or injustice, write it down and look at it again after a week!'

'The best advice I ever had was to forget about revenge. For some reason I felt a need to get my own back and I've realised that's not uncommon. Don't waste your own or the family's time and energy. Just get on with it. Coping with it is the best revenge.'

Advice on coping with, organising and managing different aspects of dyslexia has been the focus of this chapter which collates parents' responses to item 4 of the questionnaire. It is hoped that parents newly coming to terms with their child's innate difficulties will benefit from the experiences of those involved in the initiative.

Chapter 5
Dealing with the practicalities: Strategies/resources/ tactics

Reference: Questionnaire item 5: Thinking of the practical, day-to-day management of dyslexia, which strategies/resources/tactics have proved useful and why?

This chapter describes various tried, tested and practical ways of dealing with dyslexia and its associated manifestations: poor organisation, limited recall, difficulties with time/space and so forth. Parents' ingenuity and initiatives were impressive but one of the simplest strategies is possibly amongst the most important:

'Immediately after she'd seen the psychologist, I drafted a brief letter which began, 'Dear Teacher'. I then photocopied it many times and every September I send a personally addressed copy to all the teachers involved in her education. I also send one to any new member of the school staff or if subject tutors change.

I did this because other parents had told me about breakdowns in communication. Apparently it's not unusual for parents to go to Open Evening and discover that some staff are unaware of the problem. If you do it my way it puts people in the picture. It also makes everyone concerned accountable.'

Draft letter

Dear Teacher,

You may have been told that my son P . . . is disabled by specific learning difficulty/dyslexia and I am now writing to confirm this.

Kindly contact either my husband or myself if there are any problems arising.

Yours sincerely,

That liaising with school is usually worthwhile goes almost without saying; parents have to sort out many school-related practicalities. Several useful ideas emerged:

'Schools tend to use a standard book for written work and he was forever getting them, and his papers mixed up. In desperation, I bought a different coloured file for each subject. I cut a tiny strip off each one and then stuck strips on the appropriate books and folders.

It saves time when he's packing his bag and he no longer turns up to, say, geography with a writing book full of history homework.'

The contentiousness of homework was mentioned frequently and several parents said that compromise had proved the most successful strategy:

'Agree on the time to be spent and set an alarm. Don't cheat by trying to coax him to do more. When the alarm goes off he should be allowed to stop immediately.

I've found that this works reasonably well and we're not always at each other's throat. In any case, I'm not sure about the value of work done under threat of punishment.'

One mother reported a more positive attitude to homework when it was done first thing in the morning:

'It's a pain but we both get up 45 minutes early. I can always find something to do and I'm on hand if he needs help. . . The house is quiet, we're both fresh and – if it's for a test that day – he's more likely to remember.'

A poor memory is typical of the dyslexic and most parents had found that easily available aids helped with maths and number work:

'Buy a pencil box with the times tables printed on the lid. It might seem like cheating but I don't think so. He can't help forgetting which number he's just said. . . I know he's good at maths and he estimates well so why shouldn't he take the drudgery out of calculation?

'Get him a calculator and show him how to get the best out of it. It's a useful thing to know in any case and it will save a lot of grief.'

One parent, on the other hand, had persevered with a times table tape[1] and found it useful. 'I kept it in the car so it was no trouble really. I just switched it on automatically. . . I suppose it was the constant repetition that did it.'

Tape-recorders can also be used for reminders/reinforcement and were recommended by a number of parents:

'Get into the habit of leaving his messages on tape; he can play it back as many times as he needs to. You need to think about what you're going to say, of course. Organise instructions according to an "Order of mention".'

'I tape any comprehension passages he has to read. He finds the playback and repetition helpful. He can read at that level but it's slow and painful and we think there are better uses for his energies.'

Post-it notes were also recommended, a particular strategy being explained by a foster parent who participated in the survey:

'We bought lots of pads of different coloured Post-it notes and each child picked a colour. We stick them on the inside of the front door. It's become a routine: first job every morning is to check if there's a message for you – it can be a reminder about taking something to school or just anything. It's obviously better if the child's a reasonable reader but it's amazing what can be done with pictures and diagrams once you get the hang of it.'

Another small aid which featured in almost every answer was the Franklin Spellmaster. In addition to the fun of playing its word

---

[1]   *Tables. Disco.* Webucational, Wimborne, Dorset.
    Multiplication Tables. Cadence Cassettes, Totton, Southampton.

games, it is said to be useful for – amongst other things – spelling and dictionary work.

More expensive items were also said to have been a good investment:

'The computer is the best thing we ever bought but you need to make sure you get the right one. We were interested in the word-processing facility and spellchecker but nearly got talked into a much fancier package. The first chap we saw tried to sell us something that had all sorts of options but we were never going to use them. I believe that the visual/spatial dimension of the keyboard and screen helps dyslexics.

What we've got works for us because his handwriting and spelling are poor and the word-processing package has improved presentation. It's also given him a lot more confidence and – because it slows him down – we feel the spelling has got better.'

Lap-top computers also featured in more than half the answers to this question, the following response being fairly representative:

'We bought an Amstrad Notepad Computer and it's just about right for us. We bought it mainly for the spellchecker but the whole family gets some use out of the Address Book and Alarm. You do need access to a printer but school's been very good about that.'

That dyslexics generally have difficulty with time/space/direction is well known and several practical tips were forthcoming:

'We bought him a Timex watch. The "past" half's in red and the "to" half in blue; that was a real help when he was learning to tell the time.'

'A watch with Arabic (rather than Roman) numbers, clear dates and an alarm has been worth its weight in gold. Apart from the obvious practical aspects, the alarm has "saved his bacon" and preserved our sanity on numerous occasions; if he has to be in by a certain time I make sure he sets the alarm and then we all know what time he's expected home. It works well.'

'Get him a year planner and help him mark off important dates, birthdays, that sort of thing. We talked about the seasons and the weather as we did it the first time and I believe that was the beginning of understanding so far as time was concerned.'

This mother also described how she had started to teach orientation:

'I gave him a strategy for left and right and kept checking that he remembered. I told him that his watch would *always, always* go on his left hand and I still check regularly, even when he's not wearing it.

I suppose that's the best strategy I've found. Once he's learned something, KEEP CHECKING AND REMINDING. They forget so easily and if they don't remember it, you may as well not have bothered in the first place. They do remember if you practise enough. I know that's how it works for spelling and it seems to work for practical things as well.'

Given the dyslexic's inherent difficulties, poor practical organisation skills are almost inevitable. All families said that domestic organisation was a problem but again, some initiatives were reported to work well. Two mothers mentioned clothes and dressing:

'When it comes to footwear I avoid anything with laces; those high modern boots with lots of laceholes are a disaster waiting to happen. If he had those, he'd either get the laces in the wrong holes (and we'd have tears) or he'd just give up and trip up. He's learned to like anything that fastens with Velcro and, whenever possible, flip-flops. I also avoid anything double-breasted and try to buy sweaters which have a very obvious front and back – a patterned front and plain back is good.'

'Don't just tell him how to organise his clothes, show him. Help him set them out, in the same order, five or six times at least. If there are variations for Winter/Summer, talk about the changes and decide what the new order should be. Then rehearse it so that he puts everything on as it should be. Before I'd come to this strategy, we'd had vests on top of pullovers and all sorts of strange combinations.'

Untidiness is a mundane – but important – fact of the dyslexic's domestic life. It appears to be a general and on-going problem, though a few successes were reported:

'My best tactic has been to insist that everything belonging to him goes home to his bedroom every night. It was hard to insist on that at first but I persisted and it's been worth it. I'm happy with the rest of the house and his room is his responsibility. If he wants it cleaned or dusted *he* has to clear all surfaces. Agreeing to this has meant a lot less rows in our house.'

'Get hold of a few big jars, the largest size pickled onion jars are best. Use them to store those bits and pieces you find all over the house. It works because you can see what's in and no one can be accused of disposing of vital treasure!'

Not least mentioned were the resources provided and/or recommended by the British Dyslexia Asscociation. The following replies were typical:

'The BDA's got a leaflet for everything, young children through to adult dyslexics. We found the one advising about examination concessions really useful.'

'The 20p I spent on the one called *Dyslexia and the Young Child* was one of the best investments I ever made. Apart from anything else, it gave me the confidence to go into school. I had something, written by an expert, which described the signs no one else had noticed. Something in writing made all the difference to my confidence and determination.'

'I like the *Guidelines for Parents* best. I don't get involved with the teaching but we do play the recommended games, often in the car. It's surprising how much you can do to help once someone's given you the ideas and the reason for doing something. I've sent for a few leaflets over the years.'

A relatively new resource was mentioned by a number of parents. The coloured filters discussed in the *Optometric Quarterly* [1] apparently help some children. 'He definitely reads better when he uses it. He's more fluent and *he* says it stops the print wobbling. I was sceptical myself at first but it does seem to help.'

That there exists some overlap between dyslexia and what is called Scotopic Sensitivity Syndrome appears to be agreed. Even more firmly established though is the popularity of *Alpha to Omega* [2], Hornsby and Shear, a language programme designed specifically for dyslexics. Almost every parent in this survey was familiar with

---

[1]   *Optometric Quaterly*, XIII, 95, British College of Optomerists.
[2]   Hornsby, B. and Shear, F., *Alpha to Omega*, Heinemann.

Hornsby's phonetic, linguistic approach to the teaching of reading, writing, speech and spelling.

> 'When the teacher first sent it home I couldn't make head nor tail of it; it just didn't make any sense but I kept looking at it and reading bits and eventually I saw what it was driving at. Once you get the basic idea, you realise how sensible – and simple – it is.'

> 'It's changed the way I think about spelling and I know I'm more help to her now. I don't do the teaching, as such, but I support more effectively. I know to group words in families and I invent things for different words. We all use the "Alpha" trick for spelling NECESSARY. '

Finally, and on a rather lighter note, one father said that the Roald Dahl books had been – and were – his favourite resource. He explained his choice:

> 'He actually laughed out loud when I read them to him and because he enjoyed them he was determined to learn to read. I don't know whether that's what you'd call useful but that's what it's all about as far as I can see.'

It would be difficult to quarrel with either these sentiments or any of the many recommendations reported earlier in this chapter. That the parents involved in the survey have probably spent a more than average amount of time, energy and capital on resources and initiatives is clear. Equally obvious – but rarely expressed – was their satisfaction in having found ways of managing this complex and frustrating syndrome.

Questions and responses: Conclusions

That families involved in both the survey and its piloting were generous with their time, energy and interest must be plain. Hopefully, their experiences will help other parents, especially those newly coming to terms with the syndrome commonly known as dyslexia.

Presumably, at the very least, some parents will begin to realise that their situation is not unique and also that their perceptions and intuitions are probably sound. They will almost certainly recognise not only the signs and symptoms described but also many of the fears and frustrations.

It appears that dyslexia can cause both stress and distress for all concerned. Nevertheless, it seems that the syndrome can be managed reasonably well and that there are tried and tested solutions to many of the associated problems. Indeed, most of the participating families appeared to have come to terms with this relatively rare and often misunderstood disability.

Moving on to the mechanics of the enterprise – the questions and commentary – it is impossible to say whether the questions were the right ones or whether the best use was made of responses. All I can say is that I have tried to exclude irrelevancies and to intrude on parents' responses only where appropriate. Finally, and as mentioned earlier, although this was never intended to be a reference or research text it is an honest attempt to describe and explain the reality of dealing with dyslexia.

Section Two

Introduction: Guidelines and activities

As mentioned in the Foreword, the terms of reference for this second section are very simple: it is a basic and broad-based First Aid package, suitable for a wide range of dyslexics. (If the student can *blend* [/c/a/t/ makes cat] and *discriminate* [the separate sounds in cat are /c/, /a/, /t/] between sounds, the activities are unlikely to do any harm and will very probably be beneficial.) However, the package is not a substitute for a full and detailed teaching programme but a practical response to expressed needs.

The material is organised according to the principles which usually inform the remedial programmes recommended for dyslexics. The package is designed to help with both reading and spelling. It is structured, cumulative and progressive, the order of presentation following that of the provenly effective *Alpha to Omega*[1]. The photocopiable word-searches and Ladders games complement the Guidelines. Users will notice that success is built-in to the activities and that repetition and reinforcement are priorities. This is deliberate and not necessarily boring given an inventive and inspiring approach.

Supervising parents and teachers might also find the Edith Norrie Letter Case[2] useful. This piece of equipment provides a multi-sensory approach to the problems of dyslexia and its use would probably make the basic package that much more effective. (Pupils might use the individual letter tiles to make the words used in the Word Searches and Ladders games, for example.)

Lastly, it must be said that the unpublished version of this package has been in use for a very long time. It has been welcomed and found effective by dyslexics of all ages, hence its inclusion in this book.

[1]   Hornsby, B. and Shear, F. *Alpha to Omega*, Heinemann.
[2]   Available from Helen Arkell Dyslexia Centre, Frensham, Farnham, Surrey GU10 3BW

Ladders game

Basically, the usual rules for Snakes and Ladders apply. Each game could be played by several players but is probably more effective when played by a pupil and a teacher. Each player needs a counter, pencil and writing pad. A dice and egg-cup are also required.

Instructions for playing:

1. The pupil shakes the dice first and counts off the boxes (□) according to the number shaken. For example: if, in game 1a), the pupil shakes a 4, he will land on the fourth box (c-n). He then has to write his word (*can*), sounding and blending as he writes.[1]
2. If the pupil cannot then read the word or writes it incorrectly, he forfeits his next turn.
3. Instructions regarding the symbols entered in the boxes (✻) (☛) are noted on each sheet.
4. The arrows on the ladders indicate moves upwards and downwards and two words have to be written when these routes are followed.
5. The other player/teacher repeats the procedure and so on until one of the players reaches FINISH.

Guidelines

1. Every English word (and every syllable) must have a vowel or the letter *y* acting as a vowel. A single vowel 'trapped' between two consonants is usually short as in p*a*t, p*e*t, p*i*t, p*o*t, p*u*t.
   See also: Word Searches 1a, 1b, 1c, 1d, 1e and Ladders 1a, 1b, 1c, 1d, 1e.
2. When *ed* is added to a basic (or root) word, it sometimes sounds like *t* as in jump*ed*.
   See also: Word Search 2 and Ladders 2.
3. The letter *w* may also cause confusion. It can be silent (as in *w*rap). It can change the sound of the letter following as in *w*ash.
   See also: Word Searches 3a and 3b and Ladders 3a and 3b.

---

[1] These games may be unsuitable for pupils who cannot blend and discriminate between sounds.

4.   A silent final *e* opens a syllable (or word) and usually makes the previous vowel say its name in the alphabet. Example: g*ame*, h*ere*, t*ime*, r*ope*, t*ube*: dict*ate*, athl*ete*, desp*ite*, cons*ole*, ref*use*.
     See also: Word Searches 4a, 4b, 4c, 4d, 4e and Ladders 4.

5.   English words cannot end in *v*: *–ve* is used.
     See also: Word Search 5 and Ladders 5.

6.   The letter *c* is sometimes used instead of *s*, most commonly when it is followed by *e* as in *ce*ntre or ri*ce*.
     See also: Word Searches 6a and 6b and Ladders 6a and 6b.
     (The letters *i* and *y* have the same effect on *c* but words with this combination are rather less common.)

7.   English words cannot end *j*: *– dge* is usually used immediately after a short vowel, otherwise *– ge*.
     See also: Word Searches 7a and 7b and Ladders 7a and 7b.

8.   *age* is usually sounded like *ij*, when it appears at the end of a longer word.
     See also: Word Search 8 and Ladders 8.

9.   English words very rarely end in *i*. The letter *y* is used instead.
     See also: Word Searches 9a and 9b and Ladders 9a and 9b.

10. When vowels appear in pairs (*ai, oa, ea*, etc.), the second vowel is often 'silent' while the first vowel says its name in the alphabet. Examples: r*ai*d, r*oa*d, r*ea*d.
     See also: Word Searches 10a, 10b, 10c and Ladders 10a, 10b, 10c.

Word Search 1a
Guideline 1

A single vowel trapped between two consonants is usually short as in
p*a*t, p*e*t, p*i*t, p*o*t, p*u*t.

Find and circle:

fan , man, pan, ran, tan, van
x2   x2   x2   x2   x2   x2

f	a	n	b	q	s	z	y	p	m	x
a	p	a	n	r	m	a	n	q	b	r
b	j	a	c	r	a	n	v	s	l	e
r	a	n	d	p	h	i	c	f	a	n
c	k	z	t	a	n	w	t	u	q	d
d	m	y	e	o	t	l	k	u	v	x
e	v	a	n	n	u	d	h	k	g	l
f	n	x	f	m	t	a	n	g	x	i
g	o	w	g	p	v	o	n	w	k	h
p	a	v	h	l	y	g	p	a	n	x
r	q	v	a	n	l	h	w	q	p	x
s	t	u	i	p	k	x	w	g	z	m
m	a	n	j	k	i	d	l	x	w	k

Word Search 1b
Guideline 1

A single vowel trapped between two consonants is usually short as in p*a*t, p*e*t, p*i*t, p*o*t, p*u*t.

Find and circle:

get, let, met, net, pet, vet
x2   x2   x2   x2   x2   x2

→

g	e	t	a	m	e	t	r	h	m	v
u	z	h	u	q	z	s	j	y	e	g
u	k	w	n	e	t	p	k	m	n	a
n	k	z	n	h	s	x	n	z	w	q
t	m	e	t	j	h	n	b	p	e	t
w	q	n	m	p	e	t	k	g	u	d
v	e	t	n	z	k	u	h	z	f	z
z	w	z	c	j	h	u	r	u	k	p
n	e	t	w	k	d	n	j	l	w	v
c	z	f	p	v	j	r	g	e	t	p
k	a	z	z	l	e	t	b	f	w	j
z	r	f	d	v	j	v	e	t	n	v
a	l	e	t	f	u	a	w	u	u	z

Word Search 1c
Guideline 1

A single vowel trapped between two consonants is usually short as in pat, pet, pit, pot, put.

Find and circle:

lip,   nip,   pip,   rip,   sip,   tip
x2   x2   x2   x2   x2   x2

→

l	i	p	q	z	u	l	n	x	f	m
n	g	f	y	q	p	i	p	l	u	z
m	s	i	p	n	x	n	i	p	y	g
f	q	t	h	l	m	n	b	d	u	o
n	s	w	l	d	w	y	r	i	p	i
o	s	i	p	x	z	g	h	d	t	z
q	m	w	n	i	p	y	o	u	w	o
z	t	q	o	b	m	g	t	i	p	y
m	f	h	r	i	p	l	n	f	d	m
y	l	i	p	q	s	n	b	u	h	s
g	d	h	f	x	g	l	h	s	f	t
p	i	p	t	d	z	g	u	y	l	d
m	x	u	v	l	n	t	i	p	q	x

Word Search 1d
Guideline 1

A single vowel trapped between two consonants is usually short as in pat, pet, pit, pot, put.

Find and circle:

cot, got, hot, lot, not, pot
x2   x2   x2   x2   x2   x2

→

a	q	c	o	t	d	f	h	j	n	o
g	o	t	z	x	h	r	e	o	p	i
w	z	x	q	m	w	g	o	t	q	x
k	m	d	k	h	o	t	m	q	x	t
q	d	z	k	x	w	p	o	t	m	t
e	l	o	t	z	p	l	v	l	t	d
x	z	w	p	o	t	v	t	s	e	w
d	q	s	z	w	z	n	o	t	b	d
p	d	e	x	p	d	l	t	k	d	v
s	k	c	o	t	l	x	t	p	k	s
p	q	w	e	z	x	l	h	o	t	d
v	s	k	e	v	n	o	t	m	p	x
l	o	t	k	z	e	x	l	k	z	l

Word Search 1e
Guideline 1

A single vowel trapped between two consonants is usually short as in pat, pet, pit, pot, put.

Find and circle:

hug, mug, rug, tug, bug, jug
x2   x2   x2   x2   x2   x2

$\longrightarrow$

h	u	g	q	s	x	w	z	c	h	d
s	h	f	s	w	m	u	g	x	c	h
w	c	j	u	g	q	s	z	d	c	l
k	l	f	q	z	s	w	h	u	g	k
h	c	z	f	t	u	g	x	l	j	r
z	m	u	g	x	r	k	a	d	k	x
w	c	s	f	j	q	k	s	w	q	l
k	c	h	l	k	f	r	u	g	h	f
d	b	u	g	z	f	s	q	w	d	x
j	k	j	l	t	u	g	z	x	c	z
f	s	d	q	h	f	s	j	u	g	w
w	c	d	x	s	b	u	g	z	d	w
q	r	u	g	d	w	x	s	w	c	d

Word Search 2
Guideline 2

When *ed* is added to a basic (or root) word, it sometimes sounds like *t* as in jump*ed*.

Find and circle:

tossed,   crossed,   winked,   blinked,   jumped,   thumped
x2   x2   x2   x2   x2   x2

→

t	o	s	s	e	d	q	z	x	c	v
p	w	i	n	k	e	d	l	k	j	h
z	x	v	c	r	o	s	s	e	d	f
b	l	i	n	k	e	d	l	m	n	b
s	d	j	u	m	p	e	d	f	g	h
t	h	u	m	p	e	d	a	w	q	g
w	i	n	k	t	o	s	s	e	d	h
t	y	t	h	u	m	p	e	d	u	i
r	w	i	n	k	e	d	v	f	h	i
r	t	f	c	w	q	a	s	d	f	g
m	j	u	m	p	e	d	n	h	t	r
q	w	b	l	i	n	k	e	d	s	r
c	r	o	s	s	e	d	r	g	y	p

Word Search 3a
Guideline 3

The letter *w* may also cause confusion. It can be silent, as in *w*rap.

Find and circle:

wrap,   wrist,   wring,   wrong,   wreck,   wrung
x2   x2   x2   x2   x2   x2

w	r	a	p	y	p	i	u	y	t	r
f	g	h	j	w	r	o	n	g	k	l
w	r	o	n	g	m	n	b	c	x	z
w	r	i	s	t	h	g	f	d	s	a
a	s	d	f	w	r	i	s	t	t	h
m	w	r	i	n	g	x	z	k	v	p
b	h	f	w	r	e	c	k	q	w	e
d	w	r	u	n	g	f	h	g	v	c
a	x	c	v	f	g	h	g	t	y	u
w	c	s	s	w	r	u	n	g	d	h
b	n	h	y	r	d	f	g	c	x	z
s	w	r	e	c	k	h	f	q	w	v
w	r	i	n	g	m	n	w	r	a	p

Word Search 3b
Guideline 3

The letter *w* may also cause confusion. It can change the *sound* of the letter following as in *wa*sh.

Find and circle:

was,   wash,   want,   wasp,   wand,   washed
x2   x2   x2   x2   x2   x2

⟶

w	a	s	z	x	c	v	b	n	m	l
h	w	a	s	h	j	w	a	n	t	k
a	d	s	f	w	a	s	p	g	h	j
w	a	n	d	q	w	e	v	t	y	u
q	w	w	a	s	h	e	d	t	y	u
n	b	m	z	x	c	v	f	g	b	h
b	g	w	a	n	d	q	u	f	g	j
s	d	t	y	h	b	e	z	w	l	t
v	b	n	m	h	k	w	a	s	h	q
w	a	s	p	d	e	f	g	b	n	j
z	w	a	s	h	e	d	z	p	l	k
x	v	c	w	a	n	t	q	e	w	g
w	a	s	g	h	n	m	h	j	k	l

Word Search 4a
Guideline 4

A silent e opens a syllable (or word) and usually makes the previous vowel say its name in the alphabet.

Find and circle:

gate,	hate,	late,	mate,	rate,	date
x2	x2	x2	x2	x2	x2

——————————→

g	a	t	e	k	l	p	o	v	z	x
p	o	i	g	a	t	e	y	t	r	e
q	l	a	t	e	w	s	x	c	f	t
m	n	n	a	s	d	a	t	e	b	h
x	z	r	a	t	e	c	v	d	g	h
g	m	i	m	l	j	h	a	t	e	o
m	a	t	e	f	b	z	x	c	g	h
h	g	s	t	r	e	w	q	l	k	j
n	b	d	q	z	r	a	t	e	f	c
f	d	a	t	e	b	b	g	h	j	k
x	z	c	w	q	d	b	n	m	m	l
h	a	t	e	c	l	a	t	e	v	z
l	k	j	m	a	t	e	p	h	g	e

Word Search 4b
Guideline 4

A silent e opens a syllable (or word) and usually makes the previous vowel say its name in the alphabet.

Find and circle:

here,   these,   theme,   concrete,   complete,   athlete
x2   x2   x2   x2   x2   x2

→

h	e	r	e	o	a	y	c	a	o	w
a	w	t	h	e	s	e	c	y	c	t
t	h	e	s	e	i	a	y	c	g	z
c	o	n	c	r	e	t	e	a	t	c
r	z	c	o	m	p	l	e	t	e	l
a	t	h	l	e	t	e	i	c	e	c
u	f	f	w	a	x	i	t	a	y	w
e	w	a	t	h	l	e	t	e	i	a
c	o	m	p	l	e	t	e	u	a	l
t	h	e	m	e	a	h	e	r	e	f
f	u	a	w	z	u	z	a	w	g	r
c	o	n	c	r	e	t	e	x	a	g
w	u	t	h	e	m	e	w	h	a	g

Word Search 4c
Guideline 4

A single e opens a syllable (or word) and usually makes the previous vowel say its name in the alphabet.

Find and circle:

hide, ride, side, tide, wide, slide
x2   x2   x2   x2   x2   x2

→

h	i	d	e	k	h	f	h	r	q	a
w	e	h	i	d	e	j	j	w	a	p
p	g	k	d	k	z	s	i	d	e	z
s	i	d	e	f	w	t	i	d	e	z
r	k	g	a	w	r	k	h	w	z	j
p	r	w	i	d	e	u	w	w	j	k
w	i	d	e	q	m	r	i	d	e	p
q	s	l	i	d	e	n	z	g	c	o
c	w	w	e	n	m	g	k	o	p	w
z	c	k	p	s	l	i	d	e	k	c
t	o	i	w	o	z	b	k	o	k	w
c	z	o	z	s	t	i	d	e	u	t
t	c	r	i	d	e	b	b	c	k	n

Word Search 4d
Guideline 4

A silent e opens a syllable (or word) and usually makes the previous vowel say its name in the alphabet.

Find and circle:

hope,   mope,   pope,   rope,   cope,   slope
x2   x2   x2   x2   x2   x2

→

h	o	p	e	z	r	f	a	f	a	b
r	z	m	o	p	e	t	t	b	a	y
a	a	w	p	o	p	e	t	r	y	b
r	o	p	e	y	t	y	b	h	m	q
t	y	f	r	o	p	e	t	r	m	a
d	b	f	b	b	v	c	o	p	e	q
l	k	c	o	p	e	q	t	q	q	b
s	l	o	p	e	q	t	a	f	r	n
d	v	c	z	p	o	p	e	b	r	t
h	o	p	e	v	b	a	b	o	b	o
f	v	f	f	g	u	i	h	n	r	m
v	g	l	f	q	m	o	p	e	c	d
v	q	s	l	o	p	e	a	k	l	a

Word Search 4e
Guideline 4

A silent e opens a syllable (or word) and usually makes the previous vowel say its name in the alphabet.

Find and circle:

cure, pure, sure, fuse, confuse, refuse
x2   x2   x2   x2   x2   x2

→

c	u	r	e	r	v	c	u	r	e	l
v	v	c	s	u	r	e	u	m	a	l
w	s	f	u	s	e	w	v	p	n	p
c	o	n	f	u	s	e	t	e	z	n
k	z	p	v	v	c	w	p	n	k	n
s	v	v	r	e	f	u	s	e	x	k
i	w	k	i	v	f	w	c	j	n	i
s	u	r	e	w	k	v	w	j	v	p
i	r	e	f	u	s	e	n	n	i	v
x	i	w	p	u	r	e	k	c	p	i
v	w	p	c	v	x	f	u	s	e	l
i	p	u	r	e	s	k	v	n	s	k
k	c	o	n	f	u	s	e	w	z	v

Word Search 5
Guideline 5

English words cannot end in *v:* – *ve* is used.

Find and circle:

love, shove, glove, above, dove, have
x2   x2   x2   x2   x2   x2

→

l	o	v	e	a	l	o	v	e	c	b
f	q	s	x	g	s	b	n	f	g	f
m	f	g	b	q	f	b	s	f	q	x
n	g	l	o	v	e	x	n	s	h	f
p	h	b	a	b	o	v	e	g	q	n
d	o	v	e	g	b	d	o	v	e	p
f	e	h	p	s	q	b	p	i	s	q
s	e	e	h	a	v	e	f	n	i	h
e	s	h	o	v	e	h	b	p	f	p
n	n	f	e	s	h	o	v	e	i	s
s	x	g	l	o	v	e	h	g	p	b
a	b	o	v	e	e	f	l	x	f	x
q	n	p	x	h	h	a	v	e	g	b

Word Search 6a
Guideline 6

The letter *c* is sometimes used instead of *s*, most commonly when it is followed by *e* as in *c*entre or ri*c*e.

Find and circle:

lice, mice, nice, rice, price, slice
x2   x2   x2   x2   x2   x2

⟶

l	i	c	e	t	n	o	v	t	v	o
o	l	r	h	t	h	t	d	v	t	n
e	g	e	n	i	c	e	h	d	p	n
h	o	h	r	n	p	r	i	c	e	g
l	r	i	c	e	z	r	t	d	z	g
m	i	c	e	l	i	c	e	l	t	p
t	e	p	r	i	c	e	l	p	h	z
h	x	o	e	d	h	r	i	c	e	g
t	e	s	l	i	c	e	y	h	g	y
p	i	p	y	l	y	r	e	t	p	e
n	t	c	z	m	i	c	e	v	h	o
n	s	l	i	c	e	c	r	e	t	l
b	s	t	b	c	b	n	i	c	e	n

Word Search 6b
Guideline 6

The letter *c* is sometimes used instead of *s*, most commonly when it is followed by *e* as in ce*ntre* or ri*ce*.

Find and circle:

centre, central, recent, decent, innocent, century
x2   x2   x2   x2   x2   x2

c	e	n	t	r	e	p	t	s	m	p
t	c	e	n	t	r	a	l	m	r	k
p	m	p	r	e	c	e	n	t	k	l
d	e	c	e	n	t	s	k	s	t	q
i	n	n	o	c	e	n	t	w	i	u
c	e	n	t	u	r	y	m	l	p	y
m	s	m	c	e	n	t	u	r	y	u
a	r	k	r	m	t	p	s	k	l	i
g	i	n	n	o	c	e	n	t	q	w
r	e	c	e	n	t	s	q	t	u	u
q	k	s	r	c	e	n	t	r	e	w
c	e	n	t	r	a	l	y	p	t	m
r	t	d	e	c	e	n	t	k	p	u

Word Search 7a
Guideline 7

English words cannot end in *j*: –*dge* is usually used immediately after a short vowel, otherwise *ge*.

Find and circle:

badge, hedge, sledge, bridge, lodge, judge
x2   x2   x2   x2   x2   x2

⟶

b	a	d	g	e	w	c	v	y	c	l
e	f	b	a	d	g	e	b	y	f	q
t	s	l	e	d	g	e	q	x	t	o
x	v	h	b	r	i	d	g	e	b	i
o	l	o	d	g	e	q	t	w	i	o
c	o	i	w	h	o	v	i	u	f	t
w	f	y	b	j	u	d	g	e	u	o
x	e	i	b	e	f	v	q	i	y	u
h	e	d	g	e	h	e	d	g	e	i
b	r	i	d	g	e	t	j	t	v	z
y	c	x	t	l	o	d	g	e	h	c
b	f	s	l	e	d	g	e	u	v	u
u	j	u	d	g	e	h	h	b	j	f

Word Search 7b
Guideline 7

English words cannot end in *j*: *–dge* is usually used immediately after a short vowel, otherwise *ge*.

Find and circle:

page, wage, cage, age, rage, stage
x2   x2   x2   x2   x2   x2

→

p	a	g	e	b	u	y	a	g	e	m
t	n	y	w	a	g	e	t	u	t	p
p	a	g	e	c	a	g	e	y	l	u
i	g	n	t	b	i	a	g	e	u	b
g	h	a	r	a	g	e	u	u	t	i
b	b	k	g	r	i	m	q	y	p	m
m	k	h	s	t	a	g	e	b	y	j
t	c	a	g	e	g	t	g	p	l	m
i	m	l	k	i	y	t	m	j	i	y
q	m	q	b	r	a	g	e	t	y	l
q	s	t	a	g	e	q	m	q	b	i
b	b	y	q	m	y	h	y	q	q	k
q	m	m	w	a	g	e	h	b	b	i

Word Search 8
Guideline 8

age is usually sounded like *ÿ*, when it appears at the end of a longer word.

Find and circle:

cottage, message, luggage, passage, village, cabbage
x2   x2   x2   x2   x2   x2

→

c	o	t	t	a	g	e	u	s	u	h
r	o	m	e	s	s	a	g	e	h	f
m	e	s	s	a	g	e	s	u	o	h
j	p	a	s	s	a	g	e	o	u	g
x	u	s	p	a	s	s	a	g	e	o
j	c	a	b	b	a	g	e	f	o	h
a	u	y	c	o	t	t	a	g	e	g
l	u	g	g	a	g	e	g	u	a	e
e	c	a	b	b	a	g	e	x	u	a
u	f	u	g	h	o	j	u	j	g	a
o	a	v	i	l	l	a	g	e	o	g
v	i	l	l	a	g	e	u	y	u	g
o	j	l	u	g	g	a	g	e	r	f

Word Search 9a
Guideline 9

English words very rarely end in *i*. The letter *y* is used instead.

Find and circle:

pity, very, copy, study, lily, envy
x2   x2   x2   x2   x2 x2

→

p	i	t	y	r	g	i	g	x	r	g
i	h	p	i	t	y	s	c	o	p	y
h	s	t	u	d	y	r	s	h	r	x
v	g	s	r	i	o	i	p	r	r	i
v	r	s	i	s	j	c	o	p	y	i
g	z	r	x	e	n	v	y	n	h	r
v	e	r	y	u	n	n	z	r	c	v
u	b	b	h	s	t	u	d	y	c	i
b	r	u	i	h	b	r	d	x	r	z
x	l	i	l	y	v	e	r	y	c	r
x	g	n	u	v	i	n	j	r	b	r
j	j	r	r	u	x	l	i	l	y	j
r	e	n	v	y	x	h	r	z	b	b

Word Search 9b
Guideline 9

English words very rarely end in *i*. The letter *y* is used instead.

Find and circle:

cry, dry, fly, shy, fry, sky
x2   x2   x2   x2   x2   x2

→

c	r	y	c	r	y	z	c	g	g	k
o	g	s	e	d	r	y	z	o	e	g
c	d	b	h	f	l	y	e	g	m	p
d	r	y	g	p	w	m	e	p	w	m
o	e	u	b	z	o	u	z	n	e	i
f	w	b	o	f	v	f	l	y	h	m
o	s	h	y	p	j	r	h	m	e	n
a	j	a	o	n	m	s	s	k	y	p
m	b	s	f	g	j	w	o	n	o	o
j	n	z	f	r	y	g	b	n	g	b
f	r	y	x	p	n	b	m	t	x	b
p	l	j	p	s	k	y	o	m	h	m
n	g	p	l	b	v	p	s	h	y	b

Word Search 10a
Guideline 10

When vowels appear in pairs (*ai, oa, ea,* etc.), the second vowel is often silent, whilst the first vowel says its name in the alphabet.

/A/ /O/ /E/

Examples: r*ai*d, r*oa*d, r*ea*d.

Find and circle:

raid, paid, afraid, rain, pain, train
x2   x2   x2   x2   x2   x2

→

r	a	i	d	c	r	h	r	h	f	h
s	f	z	r	a	i	d	p	a	i	d
w	s	l	f	z	s	w	z	f	z	f
a	f	r	a	i	d	l	s	h	z	w
p	a	i	d	h	f	r	a	i	n	f
w	s	y	r	a	i	n	t	z	f	f
z	p	a	i	n	h	l	l	z	s	r
y	h	y	s	w	t	r	a	i	n	s
s	o	h	f	w	s	o	p	a	i	n
o	z	g	a	f	r	a	i	d	s	r
w	t	r	a	i	n	o	s	w	s	o
w	o	g	o	h	l	f	s	l	h	o
g	o	h	o	g	g	h	f	z	l	f

Word Search 10b
Guideline 10

When vowels appear in pairs (*ai, oa, ea*, etc.), the second vowel is often silent, whereas the first vowel says its name in the alphabet.

/A/ /O/ /E/

Examples: r*ai*d, r*oa*d, r*ea*d.

Find and circle:

road, toad, coat, boat, coal, goal
x2   x2   x2   x2   x2   x2

r	o	a	d	r	j	z	i	p	z	p
z	q	c	i	m	t	o	a	d	p	m
z	i	l	z	c	o	a	t	m	p	j
c	o	a	t	m	k	n	j	m	i	p
a	i	k	m	j	q	m	z	i	p	a
c	k	j	c	i	c	b	o	a	t	z
a	c	o	a	l	i	k	i	q	i	a
c	a	p	g	o	a	l	k	j	p	c
j	m	j	b	a	i	c	i	p	p	i
b	b	m	q	j	c	o	a	l	q	j
t	o	a	d	r	o	a	d	n	i	c
b	p	q	m	b	o	a	t	c	j	q
p	q	g	o	a	l	m	n	i	c	q

Word Search 10c
Guideline 10

When vowels appear in pairs (*ai, oa, ea,* etc.), the second vowel is often silent, whereas the first vowel says its name in the alphabet.
          /A/ /O/ /E/
Examples: r*ai*d, r*oa*d, r*ea*d.

Find and circle:

read, lead, dream, cream, meal, steal
x2   x2   x2   x2   x2   x2

r	e	a	d	t	z	q	o	t	y	q
q	o	c	y	e	l	e	a	d	l	y
b	n	q	c	r	e	a	m	k	l	k
r	e	a	d	z	l	o	j	h	g	y
b	n	r	l	e	a	d	e	z	e	c
d	r	e	a	m	k	k	o	y	b	z
c	z	a	n	a	c	r	e	a	m	b
c	m	e	a	l	a	z	b	o	g	z
z	b	y	k	k	d	m	e	a	l	c
z	s	t	e	a	l	k	o	g	l	c
e	y	b	y	y	b	o	g	z	g	z
e	z	s	t	e	a	l	g	o	y	l
f	y	c	a	d	r	e	a	m	c	g

Ladders 1a
Guideline 1

A single vowel trapped between two consonants is usually short as in p*a*t, p*e*t, p*i*t, p*o*t, p*u*t.

Make a word by adding *a*. (See also *Instructions for playing*, page 40.)

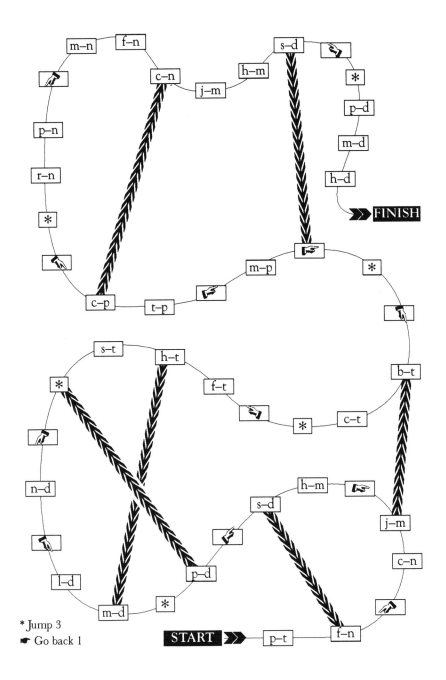

Ladders 1b
Guideline 1

A single vowel trapped between two consonants is usually short as in p*a*t, p*e*t, p*i*t, p*o*t, p*u*t.

Make a word by adding *e*. (See also *Instructions for playing*, page 40.)

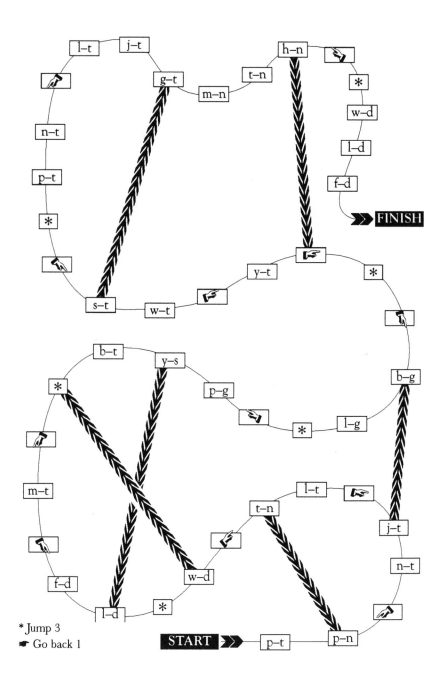

* Jump 3
☛ Go back 1

Ladders 1c
Guideline 1

A single vowel trapped between two consonants is usually short as in
p*a*t, p*e*t, p*i*t, p*o*t, p*u*t.

Make a word by adding *i*. (See also *Instructions for playing*, page 40.)

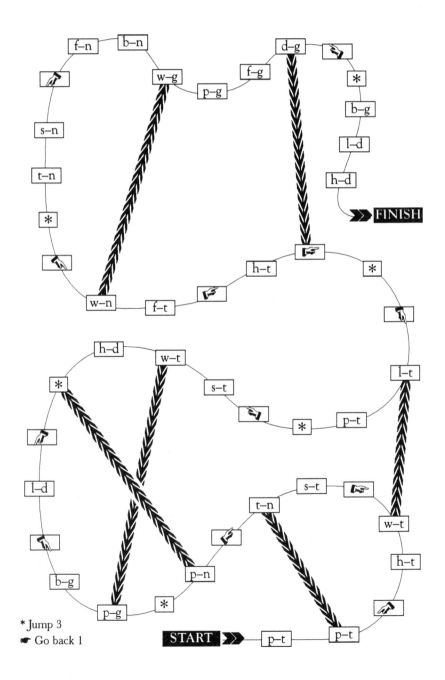

* Jump 3
☞ Go back 1

Ladders 1d
Guideline 1

A single vowel trapped between two consonants is usually short as in
p*a*t, p*e*t, p*i*t, p*o*t, p*u*t.

Make a word by adding *o*. (See also *Instructions for playing*, page 40.)

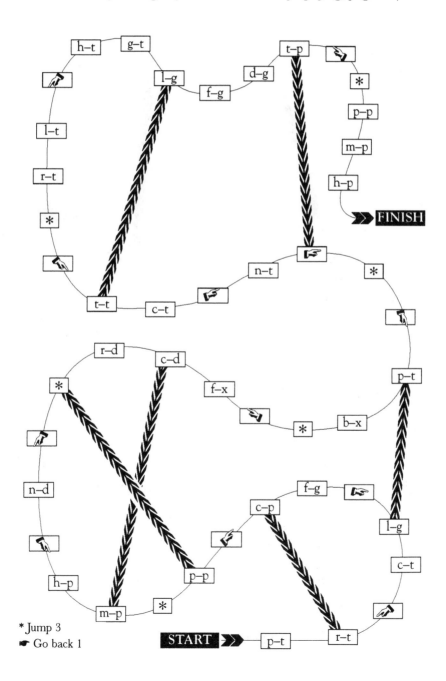

*Jump 3
☞ Go back 1

Ladders 1e
Guideline 1

A single vowel trapped between two consonants is usually short as in
p*a*t, p*e*t, p*i*t, p*o*t, p*u*t.

Make a word by adding *u*. (See also *Instructions for playing*, page 40.)

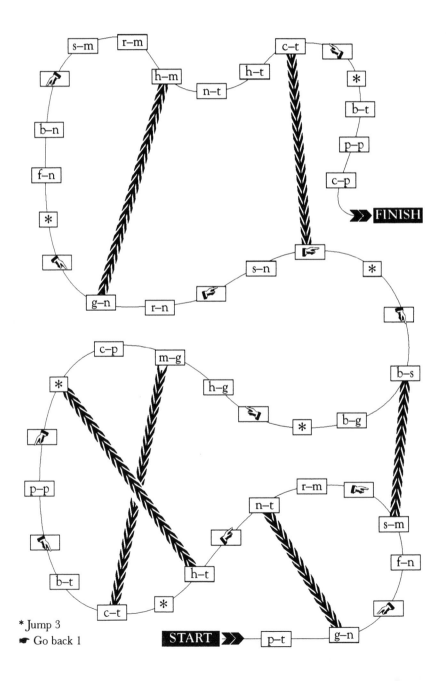

*Jump 3

☞ Go back 1

START ≫   p–t   g–n

Ladders 2
Guideline 2

When *ed* is added to a basic (or root) word, it sometimes sounds like *t* as in jump*ed*.

Make a word by adding *ed*. (See also *Instructions for playing*, page 40.)

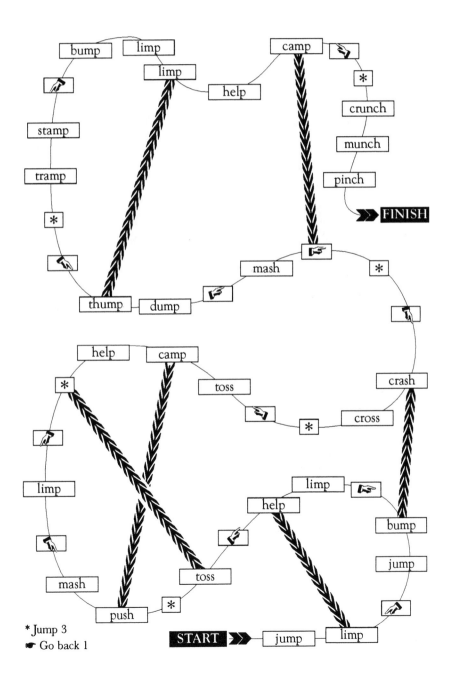

Ladders 3a
Guideline 3

The letter *w* may also cause confusion. It can be silent, as in *w*rap.

Make a word by adding *w*. (See also *Instructions for playing*, page 40.)

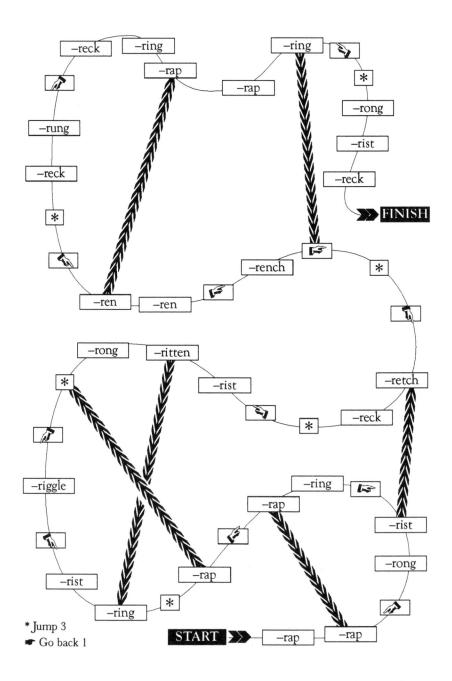

Ladders 3b
Guideline 3

The letter *w* may also cause confusion. It can change the sound of the letter following, as in *wash*.

Make a word by adding *w*. (See also *Instructions for playing*, page 40.)

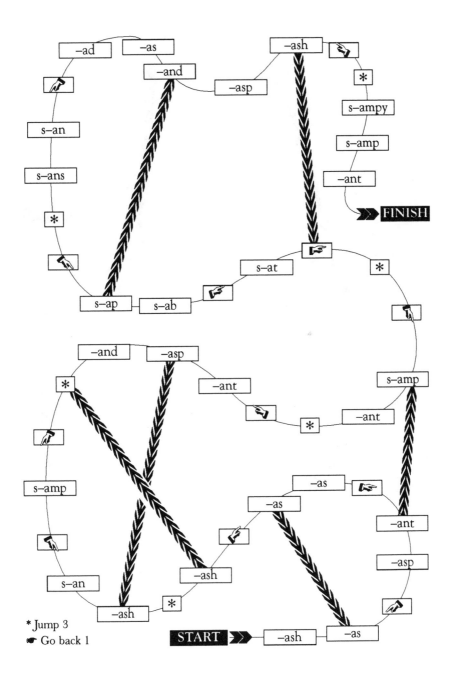

*Jump 3
☞ Go back 1

Ladders 4
Guideline 4

A silent *e* opens a syllable (or word) and usually makes the previous vowel say its name in the alphabet

Make a word by adding *e*. (See also *Instructions for playing*, page 40.)

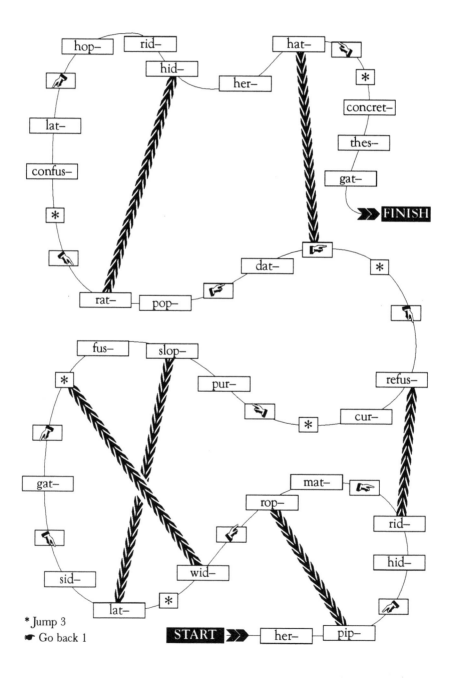

Ladders 5
Guideline 5

English words cannot end in *v*: *–ve* is used

Make a word by adding ve. (See also *Instructions for playing*, page 40.)

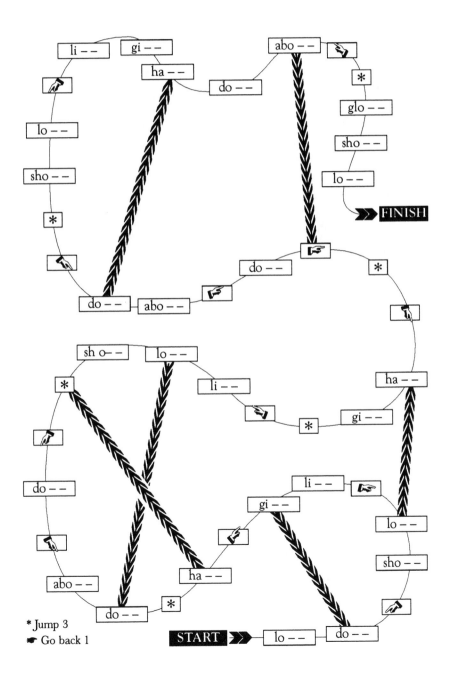

Ladders 6a
Guideline 6

The letter *c* is sometimes used instead of *s*, most commonly when it is followed by *e* as in ce*ntre* or ri*ce*

Make a word by adding *ce*. (See also *Instructions for playing*, page 40.)

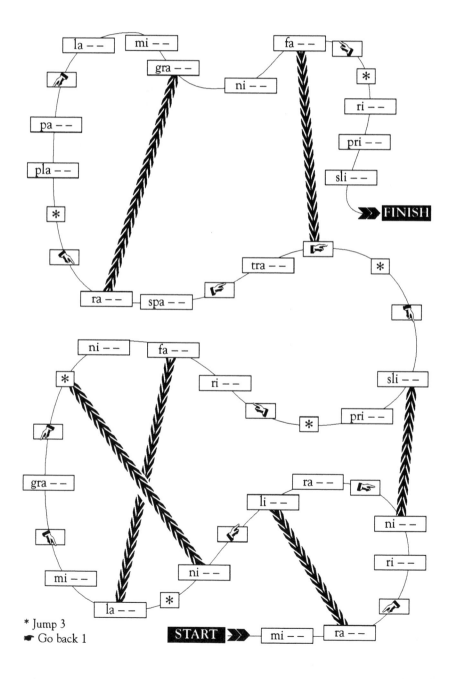

* Jump 3
☛ Go back 1

Ladders 6b
Guideline 6

The letter *c* is sometimes used instead of *s*, most commonly when it is followed by *e* as in *ce*ntre or ri*ce*.

Make a word by adding *ce*. (See also *Instructions for playing*, page 40.)

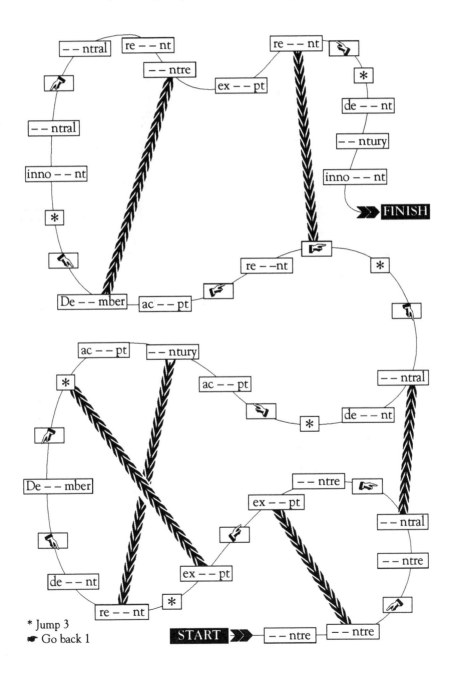

* Jump 3
☛ Go back 1

Ladders 7a
Guideline 7

English words cannot end in *j:–dge* is usually used immediately after a short vowel, otherwise *ge*.

Make a word by adding *dge*. (See also *Instructions for playing*, page 40.)

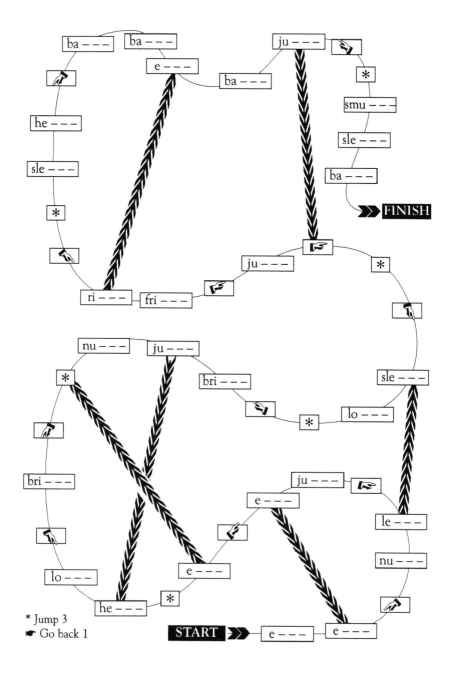

* Jump 3
☛ Go back 1

Ladders 7b
Guideline 7

English words cannot end in *j*:—*dge* is usually used immediately after a short vowel, otherwise *ge*

Make a word by adding *ge*. (See also *Instructions for playing*, page 40.)

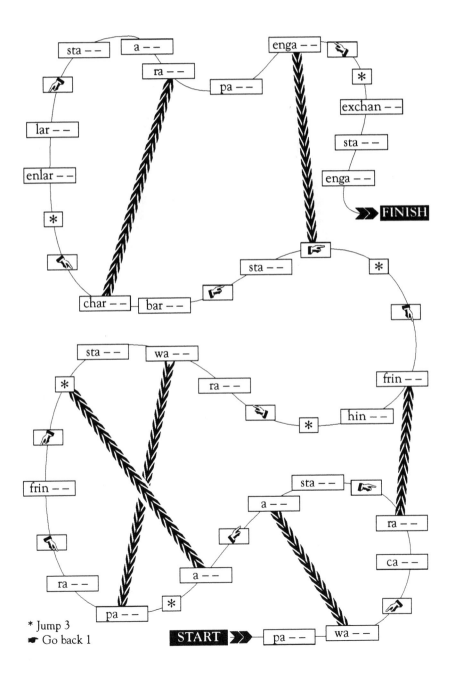

Ladders 8
Guideline 8

age is usually sounded like *ij*, when it appears at the end of a longer word.

Make a word by adding *age*. (See also *Instructions for playing*, page 40.)

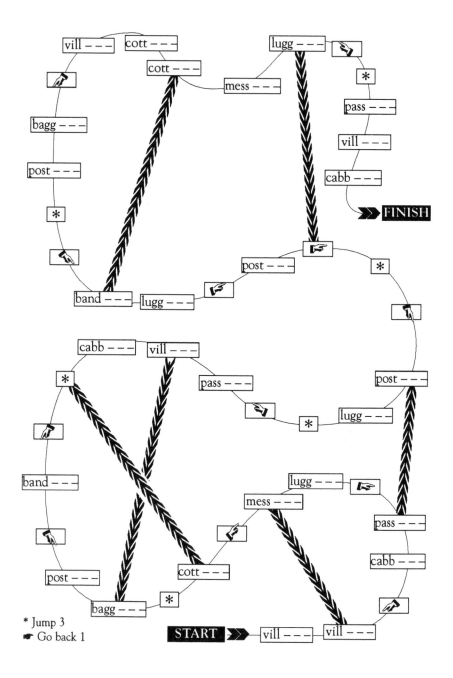

Ladders 9a
Guideline 9

English words very rarely end in *i*. The letter *y* is used instead.

Make a word by adding *y*. (See also *Instructions for playing*, page 40.)

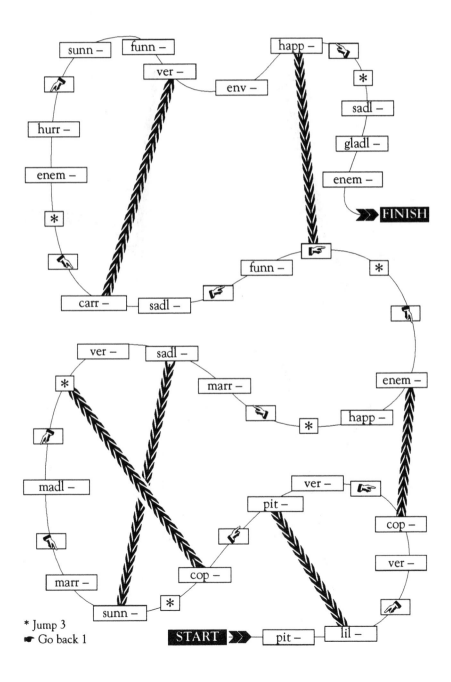

Ladders 9b
Guideline 9

English words very rarely end in *i*. The letter *y* is used instead.

Make a word by adding *y*. (See also *Instructions for playing*, page 40.)

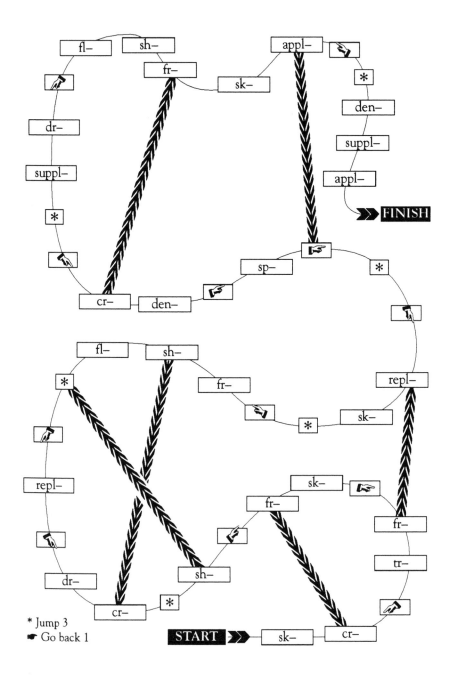

* Jump 3
☛ Go back 1

Ladders 10a
Guideline 10

When vowels appear in pairs (*ai, oa, ea,* etc.), the second vowel is often silent whilst the first vowel says its name in the alphabet. Examples: raid /A/, road/O/, read/E/.

Make a word by adding *ai.* (See also *Instructions for playing,* page 40.)

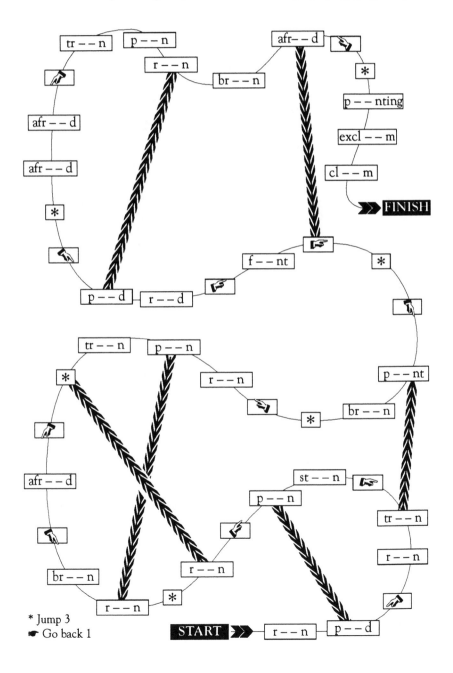

* Jump 3
☛ Go back 1

Ladders 10b
Guideline 10

When vowels appear in pairs (*ai, oa, ea,* etc), the second vowel is often silent whereas the first vowel says its name in the alphabet. Examples: raid /A/, road/O/, read/E/.

Make a word by adding *oa*. (See also *Instructions for playing*, page 40.)

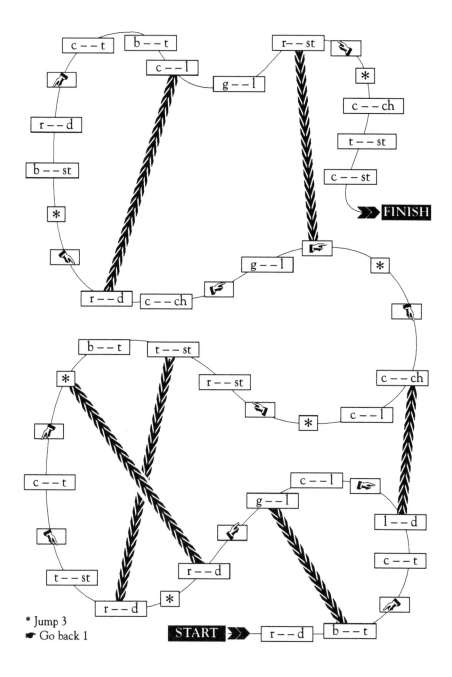

* Jump 3
☛ Go back 1

Ladders 10c
Guideline 10

When vowels appear in pairs (*ai*, *oa*, *ea*, etc.), the second vowel is often silent whereas the first vowel says its name in the alphabet. Examples: r*ai*d /A/, r*oa*d/O/, r*ea*d/E/.

Make a word by adding *ea*. (See also *Instructions for playing*, page 40.)

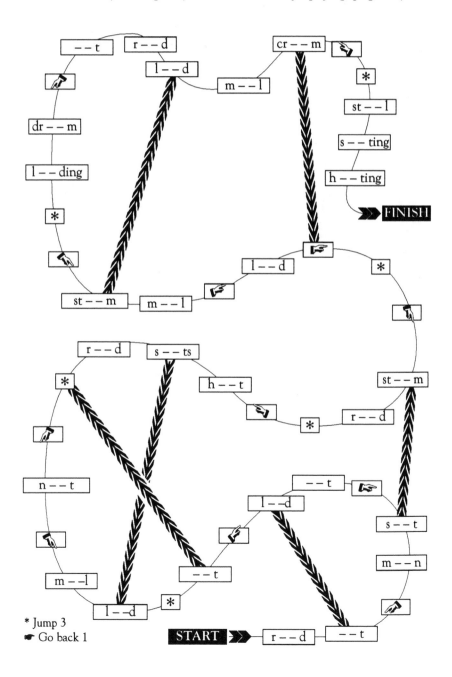

* Jump 3
☛ Go back 1

Guidelines: a final word

Although this 'First Aid' package is carefully structured, it is not a substitute for the full and detailed language programmes generally recommended for more severely disabled dyslexics. The aim here has been to provide material which appeals, at the same time introducing some of the more common linguistic concepts, rules and regularities. An understanding of the basic principles of the language is central to the dyslexic's literacy development. It is hoped that this package will at least help lay the foundations.

Postscript: Mnemonics

A comical or bizarre association of ideas improves recall and the following pages give some idea of the possibilities. Experience suggests that many dyslexic pupils are happy to invent and illustrate their own mnemonics.

Does Oliver's Egg Stink?

DOES

does

Yachts And Canoes Hunt Tuna

YACHT

yacht

Pretty red elephant's tail turns yellow

Pretty

pretty

beautiful

elephants   aren't   ugly

Four orange umbrellas repaired

Four

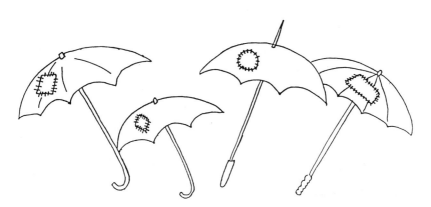

Appendix

Useful Addresses

Adult Dyslexia Organisation, 336 Brixton Road, London SW9 7AA. Telephone–0171-737-7646.

This organisation has links with adult dyslexics throughout the country. Advice about educational opportunities and resources, funding for adults and so forth is based on first-hand experience.

British Dyslexia Association, 98 London Road, Reading, Berkshire RG1 5AU. Telephone–01734-668-271

This national organisation for dyslexia/specific learning difficulties was established in 1972. The BDA has links with local organisations and can tell you your nearest point of contract. This registered charity also has leaflets on almost every aspect of dyslexia and maintains close links with other organisations/establishments, such as the Department for Education and Employment.

Local Dyslexia Associations and Support Groups are usually listed in FREE PRESS, the local library or telephone directory.
Like the British Dyslexia Association, these local groups are generally a mine of information, especially about neighbourhood schools, local provision/experiences, appeals procedures and so on. Most local associations are in regular contact with the BDA.

Dyslexia Consultancy Services (schools), 4 Arbourfield Court, Arbourfield Cross, Reading, Berkshire. Telephone–01734-760-362.

The proprieter (who is also a well-known author in the field) has extensive experience of practice and provision in both private and local education authority schools. Fees charged vary according to research/service required.

Dyslexia Institute, 133 Gresham Road, Staines. Telephone–01784-463-852.

The Institute has outposts across the country. Local institutes usually offer private assessments, teaching and teacher training. Consult local directories for further details.

CReSTeD, Council for the Registration of Schools Teaching Dyslexic Pupils, 9 Elgy Road, Gosforth, Newcastle-upon-Tyne NE3 4UU. Telephone–01395-271-633.

The CReSTeD Register may help parents to choose schools for dyslexic children. Registered schools must go through an established procedure which includes visits by a CReSTeD consultant. The main supporters of CReSTeD are the British Dyslexia Association and the Dyslexia Institute.

Helpful Books (Introductory)

Buzan T *Make the Most of Your Mind.* Pan Books.
Henderson A *Maths and Dyslexia.* Llandudno, North Wales: St David's College.
Hornsby B *Overcoming Dyslexia.* Martin Dunitz.
Miles T R (1993) *Understanding Dyslexia.* Bath: Amethyst Books.
Ostler C *Dyslexia: A Parents' Survival Guide.* Ammonite Books.
Pollock J, Waller E *Day-to-day Dyslexia in the Classroom.* Routledge.
Stirling E C *Help for the Dyslexic Adolescent.* Llandudno, North Wales: St David's College.

Helpful Books (Advanced/Academic)

Goswami U, Bryant P *Phonological Skills and Learning to Read.* Erlbaum.
Heaton, Winterson *Dealing with Dyslexia.* London: Whurr.
Pumphrey P, Reason *Specific Learning Difficulty (Dyslexia).* Routledge.
Snowling M J *Children's Written Language Difficulties.* NFER/Nelson.
Snowling M J, Thomson (Eds) *Dyslexia: Integating Theory and Practice* (BDA International Conference). London: Whurr.
Thomson M E *Development Dyslexia.* London: Whurr.

Recommended Reading Schemes

(Younger Children)

Birkett *Sounds Easy Series.* Egon.
Butterworth *The Trog Books.* Arnold.
Chaplin *The look-out gang.* Gibson and Sons.
Webster *The Shorty Series.* Ginn.

(Older Pupils/Teenagers/Adults)

Evans, Heaton *The Pam and Tom Series.* Barnsley: Barnsley College.

Language/Spelling Programmes.

Hornsby, Shear *Alpha to Omega.* Heinemann.
Hornsby *Before Alpha.* Souvenir Press.
Miles E *Syllabus; Dyslexia Unit.* Bangor, Gwynedd: University College of North Wales.
Augur J, Briggs S (Eds) (1992) *Hickey Multi-Sensory Language Course.* London: Whurr.
Hulley J *Self-Access Spelling.* National Extension College.
Pratley *Exercise Your Spelling.* BBC Publications.
Brand *Spelling Made Easy.* Egon.

Suppliers/Publishers of Material for Dyslexic Pupils

Better Books, 3 Paganel Drive, Dudley, W. Midlands DY1 4AZ.
LDA, Duke St, Wisbech, Cambs. PE13 2AE.
Learning Materials Ltd, Dixon St Wolverhampton WV2 2BX.
Special Educational Needs, 9 The Close, Church Aston, Newport, Shropshire TF10 9JL.
Whurr Publishers Ltd, 19b Compton Terrace, London N1 2UN.

Index